Julie Eschbach

THIS ROAD I'M ON

THIS ROAD I'M ON

The Power of Hope in the Face of Adversity

Bill Lee
with David Lambert

THOMAS NELSON
Since 1798

This Road I'm On

Published in Nashville, Tennessee, by Thomas Nelson. Thomas Nelson is a registered trademark of HarperCollins Christian Publishing, Inc.

The Author is represented by Ambassador Literary, Nashville, Tennessee.

Thomas Nelson titles may be purchased in bulk for educational, business, fund-raising, or sales promotional use. For information, please e-mail SpecialMarkets@ThomasNelson.com.

Library of Congress Cataloging-in-Publication Data

Library of Congress Control Number: 2018936845

ISBN 978-1-595545480 (Paperback)
ISBN 978-1-595543547 (Hardbound)
ISBN 978-1-599510187 (Custom)
ISBN 978-1-595543059 (eBook)

This book is dedicated to my beautiful wife Maria, who has been a constant source of love, devotion, and encouragement. She is God's gift to me, and I wouldn't want to travel down this road with anyone else.

As for me, I will always have hope;

  I will praise you more and more....

Though you have made me see troubles,

  many and bitter,

  you will restore my life again.

PSALM 71:14,20A NIV

CONTENTS

FOREWORD

We all know or know of people whose lives have influenced our own in outsized ways. People whose influence has been so great that we can't imagine—and don't want to imagine—how our lives might look if we hadn't known them. Decades ago at Belmont Church in Nashville, I met two of those people: Bill and Carol Ann Lee. They were about the same age as my wife Debbie and me, came from the South like us, and were equally passionate followers of Jesus.

As we continued to cross paths at church, the four of us grew ever closer. Eventually, Carol Ann and Debbie concluded that with busy husbands and babies coming fast, they wanted a group of like-minded women who would meet weekly for prayer. They invited some women to join them, and so "the Prayer Group" was born and, through the faithfulness of God, continues to this day. Not surprisingly, the women frequently pulled their men in for prayer, worship, and socializing. Some of our best and truest friends are in that group. Among them is Bill Lee, who is indeed a "friend who sticks closer than a brother" to me. Our hearts are knit tightly.

Our group prayed together through many of the joys and sorrows common to young families, but nothing prepared us for what happened on July 22, 2000. We were stunned when the news rushed through our hometown of Franklin, Tennessee, of Carol Ann's horseback riding accident. I offered Bill what support I could and so was able to observe firsthand as he summoned the courage and faith necessary to not only deal in his own heart with this blow, but also to shepherd his four kids through an experience no kids should ever have to face. I already admired Bill's strength and his simple commitment to doing the right thing. But after Carol Ann's accident, I watched that strength and commitment tested beyond endurance—and yet he endured.

I don't need to tell you any more about Bill's character—you're about to read the book, and once you have, you'll have joined the long list of people who see in Bill's life an example of how life should be lived—both when setback after crisis after catastrophe strike, and also when life allows us the freedom to choose our own direction. When Bill is given that freedom, he looks for places to serve, places to make a positive difference. And he has proven time and again that he can do just that.

In *This Road I'm On*, you'll read about Bill's childhood on the farm where he was raised and still lives today—caring for cattle, picking blackberries, cutting hay, year after year. You'll read about the long list of family crises that struck his young family and watch in awe as he and his family navigate their way through crises that would have destroyed many families. You'll watch Bill lead his family-founded and family-owned company, Lee Company, through perilous times that nearly drove them under and then to their period of greatest success and prosperity. You'll rejoice with Bill as he courts and weds his second wife, Maria. And you'll walk beside Bill as he invests himself and his resources in people and causes that make a difference: in the life of a young man from the inner city, in the life of a prison inmate being released back into society, and in the lives of the "child mothers" of northern Uganda—girls and young women abducted by the forces of Sudanese dictator Joseph Kony and handed over to his troops to use however they desired. All of us notice such needs as we walk through life and we often think, *Someone should do something about that.* Bill doesn't just talk about it: he does something.

Because this book fairly represents Bill's life and heart, you will be helped, and you will be changed. I know, because his life has inspired, helped, and changed me.

May this book do the same for you.

Michael W. Smith
Nashville, Tennessee

Acknowledgments

From Bill:

I want to thank those who have made it possible for me to write this book.

To Maria, who has worked as hard as I have on the project and who has actually become the most important part of my story.

To my kids, Jessica, Jacob, Caleb, and Sarah Kate, for whom this story is the most painful of all. Their willingness to allow it to be told, for their lives to be exposed in the hope of helping others, has been an inspiring thing for their dad to observe.

To Wes Yoder, who inspired me originally to write a book, and Dave Lambert who worked tirelessly with me for months to be certain the story was told in my voice.

To Andrew Miller, my close friend who read and reread manuscripts and used his gifts to add greatly to the final outcome.

And finally I want to express gratitude to the true author of my story, the one who created me and walked alongside me through every word written in the book that is my life and who will never leave nor forsake me until I see him face to face.

From Dave:

Thanks to Cindy, my wife, for her patience and understanding as I've put in the long hours and seven-day weeks that are often necessary to create a book like this. Fortunately Cindy's a writer too, so she understands. Since I'm writing this on Valentine's Day, it seems entirely appropriate to say: I love you.

And thanks to my colleagues at our little publishing services bureau Somersault for "loaning" me to this project for several months. I'll make it up to you.

Thanks also to Bill Lee and Wes Yoder for being willing to include me in *This Road I'm On*. Hard work, but I've enjoyed every minute, and count myself the richer for it. As the book's first reader, I can tell all who come to it after me: Bill's story will tear you up—and then put you back together better than before.

And to Sarah, my own Jessica. I love hard stories with happy endings.

CHAPTER 1

MOUNTAIN GOATS AND THE UNIMAGINABLE

In the summer of 1979, Carol Ann Person (pronounced Per-*sahn*) worked in Yellowstone National Park driving a truck filled with crates of soft drinks and refilling vending machines. I spent time backpacking in the park that summer. Even though we didn't meet until we returned to Auburn University in the fall, we spent much of our first date talking about Yellowstone and the West in general and our love for it.

Fast forward to our sixteenth wedding anniversary. We had in the intervening years made a couple of trips to Yellowstone and the Tetons. And we'd often said, half-joking, "Someday let's rent a big old RV and take the kids on a trip out to Yellowstone." We weren't RV people—we didn't like the idea of spending our vacation encased in a gas-guzzling RV complete with television and showers and refrigeration and recliners. In fact, we poked fun at those who vacationed in RVs. We were backpackers. We were naturalists. We didn't want to just *see* the natural world through an RV window. We wanted to smell the sharp, always surprising fragrance of the sagebrush, touch the Indian paintbrush, hear the meadowlark's song, feel the sand and gravel beneath our Vibram soles, feel the change in texture of the air out West compared to the South.

As our anniversary approached, we thought, *Now or never.* We reserved an RV and invited Carol Ann's sister Elaine and her three kids to accompany us. When the big day came, I pulled that bus-sized RV up next to the house and we loaded an indefensible amount of gear—sleeping bags, clothes, and maps, of course, and even walkie-talkies, along with plenty of toys and sporting equipment. Then the ten of us—Carol Ann and I and our four kids plus Carol Ann's sister and her three— headed out in the rented RV pulling a Suburban behind us, on a two-week trip to Yellowstone and the Tetons, a place we thought we could never experience often enough.

And it was the best trip ever. It was everything we had envisioned and then some. Three adults, seven over-the-top-excited kids. Since we were essentially self-sufficient we could stay wherever we wanted, so we spent the nights wherever we happened to be when dinnertime arrived—RV campgrounds, rest stops, wherever.

And then came Yellowstone. We toured the whole park— all the major tourist attractions—Old Faithful, Grand Canyon of the Yellowstone, every geyser basin and waterfall—and lots of the less well-known spots that Carol Ann and I knew about because of our times spent in the park in years past. Then came the Tetons. In Jackson Hole, we took the kids on one of those teepee cookout adventures—riding in horse-drawn covered wagons up to the campsite while fake Indians ran through the woods around us and then attacked the chuckwagon—and joined us for dinner. It was great—the kids loved it. We took them on a long horseback trip, we rafted down the Snake—we did it all.

And when it was time to circle back toward the east again, we left Yellowstone Park via the northeast entrance, toward Red Lodge, Montana, planning to make a few more stops in South Dakota, including Mt. Rushmore. Between the park and Red Lodge, you cross Beartooth Pass.

Beartooth Pass area is, in my opinion, one of the most spectacularly beautiful spots in the country. The entire plateau around it is high—much of it over 10,000 feet in elevation. It's above timberline or right at it, so the broken terrain is made up of rocks, streams, alpine lakes, moss, grass, glaciers, and occasional twisted, short, knobby firs, spruces, and pines. It's open, vast, spacious, and chilly. It gives you a bit of a *Sound of Music* moment, if Julie Andrews's famous scene in the Austrian hilltop meadows had been filmed on rocky, nearly grass-free ridges.

We drove across the plateau that day awestruck. I was driving the RV and Carol Ann was ahead of us in the Suburban. Then she called back to us on the walkie-talkie and said, "I see mountain goats! We need to stop."

As Carol Ann well knew, I have a thing about mountain goats that dates back to my first experience hunting them when I was eighteen, on a trip to the Yukon Territory east of Alaska with my dad. She'd heard me talk about them and about that trip frequently. I have a favorite print of a mountain goat hanging on a wall at home. So we all pulled over on the rocky alpine slopes where the mountain goats grazed not far off the road. We took tons of pictures. I told the kids the story—which I'd probably told them several times before—of my trip to Alaska with their papaw, where we had hunted goats just like these.

When it was time to load up and get back on the road, I took Carol Ann aside, draped my arm across her shoulders as we took one last look back at the goats and the snowy peaks and patches of spirelike alpine fir in the background. I kissed her and said, "This is one of the best days of my life. I mean, how could it get any better? We're on the trip we've dreamed of taking for years. We've got the kids with us and your sister and her three, we're in one of the world's most unique and beautiful and unspoiled spots—and we've got mountain goats too!"

She smiled.

"Our life is right where it ought to be," I said.

When we pulled away, Elaine took her turn driving the Suburban and the kids were in the back of the RV, so in the front seat it was just Carol Ann and me. After we'd driven for a while, she said, "I think there's a passage in Job about mountain goats."

I laughed. "In Job? How many people know *anything* in Job?" At least, I didn't.

But there's always a Bible nearby in our family, so she looked it up. It took her a little while but before long she said, "Here it is." And she read it to me. It's a long passage—a whole chapter or more. As she read, I became more and more attentive, struggling to hear over the road noise and the clamor of happy kids behind us. When she'd finished, I said, "Could you read that to me again, please—slowly and loudly? I think God is trying to tell me something."

And so she did:

"Brace yourself like a man;
    I will question you,
    and you shall answer me.

"Where were you when I laid the earth's foundation?
    Tell me, if you understand.
Who marked off its dimensions? Surely you know! ...

"Who shut up the sea behind doors ...
when I said, 'This far you may come and no farther;
    here is where your proud waves halt'?

"Do you know when the mountain goats give birth?"

Job 38:3-5, 8, 11, and 40:1

I was profoundly moved. And humbled, as Job himself must have been. She closed the Bible, and the two of us began to talk about how incredibly good God had been to us. The more we talked that day the more excited we got, until we were like a couple of kids: "Can you believe how well life is going for us and how well our kids are doing? All four of them?"

It was an awesome conversation. And Carol Ann and I had the sense that God was right there with us, speaking his truth into our hearts.

Two weeks later I was speeding down the road to Vanderbilt University Medical Center, chasing a Life Flight helicopter in which Carol Ann, unconscious and not expected to live, was being rushed for emergency treatment.

It had started as a good day. About 6:00 PM, I drove home after work to the farm where we and much of my extended family—siblings, nieces and nephews, my parents—still lived in one or another of the nine houses on the 1,000-acre property. I remember crossing the bridge over the river near our house. My son Jacob and a buddy of mine were fly-fishing in the river—an idyllic scene. I continued up the driveway. My other son, Caleb, was out at the cattle barn with his cousins, feeding the calves and cleaning their stalls. I waved at them and drove down to the bottom of the driveway. Carol Ann was on her horse Bar, a brown quarter horse with black legs and mane, and she had our daughter Sarah Kate, then four years old, up on the saddle in front of her. They were riding across the creek. I honked and waved, and they waved back and then started uphill across the pasture.

I went up to the house, changed clothes, and came back to the cattle barn and chatted with my son. I was vaguely aware that my brother had a pickup in the lower barn lot, doing something.

At times like these, there often comes a moment when the whole world changes, but you don't know it yet—all you know is that something in the air has changed and you are chilled, and your senses are immediately heightened. That moment for me that day started with a sound: I thought I could hear Sarah Kate crying, far away and nearly indiscernible.

I told the kids in the barn, "Y'all be quiet." And then I listened hard, and yes, I could hear my daughter's cries.

When I'd last seen her, Carol Ann had been riding up the slope from the creek toward a high pasture. This was July, so the trees were fully leafed out and I couldn't see Sarah Kate—but I could hear her across the pasture. I yelled down to my brother Steven, who was better positioned to see up the slope, "Do you see Sarah Kate? Look up the slope between the two hills."

And he said, "Yes!"

"Is she alone?"

"Yes!" he called.

I jumped into the truck and I took out across the creek and through the cattle guard. There was Sarah Kate running down through the grass, terrified and screaming. I slammed the truck to a stop near her, grabbed her up, and said, "Is Mommy okay?"

"No!" she cried. "No!"

My brother followed me up the hill in his truck. I told Sarah Kate, "You get in the truck with Uncle Steven." Then I called to him, "Get an ambulance!"

I sped up the hill until I could see Bar standing there. Carol Ann lay on the ground nearby. I skidded to a stop and jumped out of the truck. She was face down. I rolled her over. When I checked her pulse there was a weak one, and I started doing mouth-to-mouth.

She was bleeding from her mouth. That, I learned later, was an indication of the severity of the head injury she had suffered in the fall from the horse.

I don't know how long Sarah Kate had been up there with her after the injury. Nor does Sarah Kate. She, too, had hit her head in the fall and lost consciousness. She has a memory of waking up and trying to get her mom to wake up too. Then Sarah Kate tried to get back up on the horse to come for me and when she couldn't, she ran. And screamed. Four years old.

As I was giving Carol Ann CPR, my son Caleb drove up on his four-wheeler—to see me doing mouth-to-mouth on his mother, with blood all over both of us. A horrible scene.

"Caleb," I said, "you need to go back to the house."

Next came my dad, wailing in grief. "Dad," I said, "get back to the house. Just take care of the kids. They need you." It was chaos.

The ambulance came, and the EMTs took over working on her. There wasn't anything I could do so I walked up the hill and sat and prayed, watching the hectic, surreal scene playing out before me. My brother-in-law, Daniel, arrived and sat silently next to me. Next came the Life Flight helicopter. By that time, I was numb—almost paralyzed, completely overwhelmed. It was as if my whole life was a glass jar that, in one horrifying moment, had been dropped and had shattered into a million pieces, and there was no way I'd ever be able to put them all back together.

When the helicopter left, I raced back to the house. My parents had taken the kids to their house. I frantically cleaned up and started down the driveway to the hospital. But as I left, my mom drove up the driveway with my two sons. Earlier in the day, Carol Ann had taken them both to get haircuts. I can still see them hanging out of the back of Mom's car, both of them wailing—and with their fresh little buzzed heads, perhaps the last thing their mom had done for them. Crying to go with me.

I said, "You can't go with me. You just stay here with Grandmaw. I'm going to take care of your mama."

The EMTs had already determined that Sarah Kate, too, had been injured; they had taken her to the hospital with a suspected concussion.

On my way to the hospital, I did something that will sound odd. I pulled the car into a little Zippy-Mart. I walked in, and the guy behind the counter said, "How are you doin'?"

And I said, "Fine. I'm doin' good. How are you doin'?" *My wife is dying. And I'm telling the man I'm doing fine. At any given moment, someone's life is falling apart. And nobody knows.*

"I need a can of Skoal," I said.

Since I was a teenager I had chewed tobacco regularly, every day—until just a few days before all of this happened. I had quit, intending to never go back to such a dirty habit. And yet here I was, buying a can. Why not? My whole world had just crashed. Nothing mattered now.

I paid and walked out of the market. I shoved the dip in my mouth, got back in the truck, and drove on.

CHAPTER 2

BLACKBERRIES, CALVES, AND 4-H

I've always been a businessman—even as a kid I cut grass, sold things from the garden, gathered and sold black walnuts in the fall, and I picked and sold blackberries in the summer.

Almost all of my memories of picking blackberries include my mom and Mr. Linton, the farmer who lived down the road, and at least one or two of my siblings.

When you're picking blackberries the blackberry bushes are in control, and you do battle with them, along with the rest of the natural world, which is definitely out to get you. First, you don't pick blackberries whenever you want—you pick them when they're ripe, and they're ripe in the first week of July, about the hottest time of the year in Tennessee. You go out fairly early in the morning, trying to get ahead of the heat of the day. But you have to prepare—just like a knight putting on his armor before battle.

You need a coffee can, a big one. But since you had to pick with both hands, you wouldn't have a hand free to hold the can. So you would punch a hole in either side of the top of the coffee can and tie twine through it so you could hang it around your neck for the berries. There was nothing worse than the sound of a blackberry hitting the bottom of the can when you first started—*thoonk, thoonk, thoonk*—because that meant you were a long way from filling the can. When you filled your coffee can, you'd go dump the berries in a bigger bucket and start over.

Blackberries grow in thickets armed with huge thorns that are very painful if you get stuck with one, which you will many times each day you pick. The thickets are surrounded by brush and long grass, and in the South areas like that are infested with chiggers. You don't want to be scratching chigger bites for the next several days, so you protect yourself by applying gasoline around your ankles and wrists and neck to deter the chiggers from crawling underneath your clothes. You'd wear long pants and long sleeves, of course, despite the heat, because of both the briars and the chiggers. Ever had chiggers? If you have, you know that when they get past your defenses and onto your skin, I can't even politely describe the places those little buggers go to attach themselves. Think of an almost microscopic tick except that instead of sucking up juices, they feed on your skin.

Besides chiggers, you're constantly looking out for rattlesnakes. And did I mention the thorns? Fall into a blackberry patch and, even if you're protected, you're going to be in a world of hurt. By the end of three hours of picking—which is about as much as you can stand, because it's getting hot by that time of day anyway—your hands are all cut up.

Part of our berry-picking equipment was a hoe or a big stick, because the big fat berries were often out of reach. They didn't grow along the edge of the thicket—they were always further in, so we would take our hoe and beat down the brush to get to the good ones. The hoe was important for another reason, too—it's the best way to kill a rattlesnake.

As the day got hotter, we got thirstier—but we never brought water bottles with us. We just drank out of the spring. We knew where every spring on the farm was, and every creek. True or not, we thought if you were upstream from the cows, it was safe to drink.

We used to tell each other before we started, "Remember— don't eat any berries until we're done!" We would laugh about it, but the truth was, once you started eating while you were picking you'd slow down, because they tasted so good you wanted to keep eating them rather than putting them in your coffee can.

They were, though, a bit sour, and eating them at home you would want to put some sugar on them, and then there's nothing better. In blackberry season, my mom would let us have blackberries for breakfast. We would fill the bowl with blackberries and cover them with sugar and milk.

Astute businessman that I was, I would sell a gallon of blackberries for five dollars. I sold them in gallon glass jars so customers could see that all the berries were black—I wasn't sneaking any red berries in there.

It's hot and sweaty work, and you're constantly fighting thorns and chiggers and keeping an eye (and ear) out for rattlesnakes. Why would that be one of the best memories of my life? Yes, it was absolutely miserable, but don't we all do this? Experience something that can only be described at some level as miserable and then for the rest of our life look back at it with great affection? In the case of picking blackberries that's easy to explain, because the reward was really, really sweet. Not only the blackberries themselves, but being able to sell them and make money. To hold that money in my hand and know that I'd earned it myself by my hard work and I could do whatever I wanted with it.

But there's more. My mom would always save some out from those I picked and make a blackberry pie, one of my favorite things to eat—a reward for my hard work.

I still live on that same farm, and the blackberries still grow here. After Carol Ann and I got married, we continued to pick blackberries. Carol Ann would freeze some, and months later, on one of the very few days each winter when it snowed in Tennessee, she would make a blackberry cobbler. And as we and the kids sat and ate that delicious cobbler, I would tell the kids, "Remember when it was 95 degrees out with 100 percent humidity and we picked blackberries? Remember the sweat and the heat and having to find ways to avoid becoming chigger food? Now we're eating those blackberries, and they're delicious—a reminder on one of the coldest days of winter, with snow on the ground outside, that summer will be back."

My experience with blackberries both as a child and later as a parent taught me a lot about the bittersweet nature of life. Hot and cold. Good and bad. Pain and pleasure. And the longer I live, the more I see this pattern recurring. I had no way as a child picking blackberries of seeing how often it would be repeated throughout my life—or of how bitter the "bitter" part of the equation would be.

I lived right down the road from my grandfather, down the dead-end, dirt, county road that crossed the farm. Few other people lived on this road—it was very rural. So rural that we had no need for street addresses—our address was simply "Route 4." My bus ride to school each day took an hour each way. Our house was so far from the county seat that it was a long-distance telephone call.

We raised cattle. My grandfather and my father worked together in a business in downtown Nashville that my grandfather had begun long before, and they also worked the farm along with the rest of us.

When I was six, my parents and four siblings and I went on a family vacation to Florida for a week. This was the 1960s, long before cell phones and texts, so if you went away for a week, no one could reach you.

When we returned home in our station wagon, we turned up the driveway and my dad stopped to collect the mail from the mailbox on the road. He brought the mail back to the car—and then sat there, because he had found something he wasn't expecting in the mail: lots and lots of cards. He began to open them. They were sympathy cards.

I didn't understand what was happening in the front seat, but I could see that my dad was very upset by what he was reading in the mail. It was the first time I remember seeing my father cry. He was finding out, before our eyes, that his father had died.

When we got up to the house, things felt chaotic. I remember that my uncle came over. We kids didn't know what to do so like kids everywhere, we tried to make ourselves small and quiet and took refuge in routine: we carried our bags up to our rooms and began to unpack. Later, Dad came up and gathered all five of us kids into the bedroom I shared with my brother. He told us that our grandfather had gone to heaven. I looked around at my siblings because I didn't know how to act. I knew that I was feeling great turmoil and sadness—I didn't know enough to call it grief—but what was I supposed to do or say? How should I behave?

My dad's family had tried to find us on vacation to let us know. They had even gotten the Highway Patrol involved. They had put off the funeral until we got home.

Both before and after, we spent a lot of time at my grandmother's house—we usually spent the night one night a week. She would read to us. Sometimes, after Grandpa died, she would be reading a book and suddenly start crying. I didn't know why. Something in the book? Or did something trigger a memory of my grandfather? He was young when he died—in his fifties. So she was very young when he died, too—fifty-two or fifty-three, maybe.

Afterward, my father took over running the farming operation as well as running the company in town. He led a dual life. He had plenty of help on the farm, because we kids did a whole lot of the farm work. I learned how to drive when I was nine or ten years old because I had to in order to feed the cattle, and they had to be fed every afternoon in the winter. No round bales back then—only square ones. My siblings and I would drive a truck to the barn, load it up with hay, and then drive to different fields distributing it. I did that every day of my life in the winter. And loved it. I love this farming life.

But there was more to raising cattle than feeding them. Nowadays cattle wear ear tags that keep flies away, but back then we had to spray them with pesticide or the flies would eat them alive. So every two weeks in the summer, we would drive every cow we owned into corrals, then start up a tractor that would drive a hydraulic pump that sprayed the contents of a 55-gallon barrel of pesticide. I can still remember the way it smelled. We would take turns, because there were two distinct jobs. One of us would herd the cattle through chutes, single file. The other would sit up on the fence of the chute with a big rubber hose with a spray nozzle and spray chemical pesticide down on the cattle as they came through the chutes. After a while we would trade jobs. And we did this for hours every other Saturday morning in the summertime.

The flies didn't attack just the cattle. While we were trying to spray the cattle to protect them, the flies would be so thick we would have to spray each other, too. We would take turns standing still while the other would spray you with the same stuff the cattle got. We would be covered in pesticide—otherwise, we'd have been covered in flies. The thought makes me shudder now. Imagine what OSHA would say about that....

My dad had a favorite saying: "Life is short." He said it so often we made fun of him.

We had a few barns on the farm for various purposes. One was the hay barn, where every year we stacked up hundreds and hundreds of bales of hay. It was a grueling job that usually happened when it was very hot outside. I can remember, on late May afternoons before school was out for the summer, coming down the dirt road on the school bus and seeing my mother and father out in the hayfield—my mom on a baler and my father walking nearby. They had already started baling.

Yes, my mom was as much a part of the baling as any of the rest of the family. My mom can hold her own in the most sophisticated social circles, but she has never shied away from hard, manual work, or looked down on it, nor did she allow her children to. Even today at eighty-four, she sells our own beef out of the back of a truck at the local farmer's market. She's a deeply devoted mother and grandmother, and was devoted to my father until the day he died in March of 2013.

By the time we got home from school on baling day, there would already be three or four hundred bales sitting in the field, with the baler still cranking them out one after the other. And as I climbed off the bus, I would think, *All of those are going to have to be picked up and put up in the hay barn before dark.*

But in rural life, people pitch in. Our neighbors would come, and we would all drive around on hay wagons loading up hay bales and taking them to the barn. We had gas-driven hay elevators sort of like a conveyor belt on a steep angle. You'd put the conveyor belt on the bed of the wagon and load hay onto the belt, which would raise it into the barn's hay loft. Others would be up in the loft, picking the bales up when they would drop off the elevator and stacking them. And how hot would the loft be while you were doing this hard work? It felt like a hundred and ten degrees. This was hard, sweaty, prickly work, and you had to stick with it till you were done.

So picture my dad out in the hay barn one day with his five kids, all of us loading hay. There was seven years' difference in age between the oldest, a sister, and the youngest—another sister. This would have been the summer just before my oldest sister went off to college. So my youngest sister would probably have been eleven. Picture the six of us working hard, hay dust in the air, sweat pouring down our faces and staining our clothes.

My dad went down to the bottom of the barn and shut off the loud conveyor. And he stood silently until he was sure all five of us were giving him our undivided attention. Then out of the sudden silence, he said, "I want you kids to never forget this moment."

My dad, of course, was a "life is short" guy.

He said, "We've worked together as a family for all these years. Taking care of cattle. Loading up the barn with hay. Hard work. And this will probably be the last time you are all together working here, on the farm. Life will change. Cynthia goes off to college this fall. People move on, find new directions. Things happen." He paused, smiled at us all, and said, "We've had a really wonderful life doing this together. So stop right now and freeze this moment in your mind. Remember it. All of us working in this barn, stacking up this hay. As miserable as it feels this afternoon, you'll look back on this one day and you will miss it, and you will remember how much it all meant to you."

Obviously, it worked. Fifty years later, I remember that moment. And he was right.

Life is short.

The farmer who worked the land adjacent to us was Cliff Linton. He was born on that farm and lived there all his life. He and his wife Mary Lou lived in a little white farmhouse. They'd never had any children, and when my parents moved nearby with five kids, the Lintons were delighted. When my own grandfather died a couple of years later, he really became like a grandfather to me.

He had an old red M model Farmall tractor with big back wheels, little front wheels, and a big metal seat. He welded a side seat to it for my brother and me to ride alongside him. Put a little seatbelt on it made out of hay twine. So I would ride along with him for hours on the side of his tractor while he clipped pastures with an old side sickle-bar clipper.

While my dad was off at work, I would spend a lot of time with Mr. Linton. We would walk down to the river and fish with little bobbers and cane poles we would cut right on the farm—tie a string on it and a hook and a little bobber and you can catch bream.

From the time I was old enough to hold a .22 rifle, Mr. Linton would also take me hunting there on the farm. Hunting, and the use of firearms, was for my family an integral part of living in the country. We had a gun cabinet full of firearms of all kinds, which our dad taught us to respect and to use safely and accurately. My dad was, like many businessmen, conservative in many ways, including in his politics, and he was a strong advocate of Second-Amendment rights—which, he explained, had to do with a lot more than hunting. I grew up knowing that we are guaranteed the right to bear arms for whatever legitimate and legal reason we needed them. Hunting is still a big part of my life. My deer stand is within walking distance of my house. All four of my children grew up hunting, both the boys and the girls.

It was Mr. Linton who taught me how to drive. He had a 1951 Chevrolet truck with a foot-button start and a stick shift up on the steering column. When I was six or seven years old, he would take me out into the middle of a pasture where I couldn't hit anything, and he would swap seats and let me drive the truck across the field. I could hardly reach the pedals, and I had to stretch up to see over the steering wheel.

By the time I was nine or ten, I could reach the pedals and was experienced enough that I could start driving on the farm. I could drive to the barn and load hay with my siblings.

I loved that '51 Chevy. As sad as I was when he sold it, though, I thought his new truck was the fanciest thing I'd ever seen in my life. He would let us sit on the back tailgate of that truck, and he'd drive us everywhere around the farm. And he loved to stomp on the gas and throw us off the tailgate. And then we'd run and catch up and try to jump back on, and when we did he'd stomp on the gas and throw us off again.

There was an old country store down the road about three miles in Fernvale. The Fernvale Grocery had a few gas pumps and a bunch of old men—retired farmers—sitting on the front porch. The stereotypical country store. Those old guys would sit there for hours. When one of them would leave, another one would come.

In the summer, we would be playing in the yard at our house and Mr. Linton would drive his truck up and stop at the end of our long driveway. He would sit there until somebody noticed he was there—because that meant he was going to the store. The first one to notice would yell, "Mr. Linton's here!" Then we would run down the driveway, jump into the back of the truck, and ride down to the store. We did this pretty much every day during the long days of summer. At the store, we would get an RC Cola and what Mr. Linton called "a piece of ice cream"—an ice-cream sandwich.

Then he would sit there for an hour or two, killing time. The river was right next to the store, so we would wander down and play in the river while Mr. Linton and his buddies sat in front of the store. We loved seeing his truck down at the bottom of our driveway every day. It meant that we could go to the store.

One other thing I learned from Mr. Linton, something he probably wouldn't be proud of: chewing tobacco. All the time I was riding along with him on his tractor, he chewed Beech-Nut tobacco. It came in plastic bags that held big twists. He'd chew off a big bite of it and stick it in his jaw. In my very earliest memories of him—fishing, to the barn, to the store—he always had a chaw of tobacco in his mouth.

So when I was about fourteen, I got some tobacco from somebody on a day my task was to take a tractor and bush-hog one of our fields—one way back and hidden from the road and the houses. As soon as I got back there, I stuck a big plug of chewing tobacco inside my cheek. I promptly got sick and threw up. And then for some strange reason, next chance I got I did it again. And again. And again. Until I got used to it and it didn't make me dizzy and sick anymore.

That was the start. And I spent forty years chewing tobacco before I managed to quit. One of my biggest regrets. I told my own children, "Please, don't chew. Why would anyone continue something that's so terrible to start that it causes your body to revolt?" Even though I said that to my kids, I *did* know why I had done it. It appeared to me, watching the adults around me such as Mr. Linton, that it was just what a man did. And at fourteen, I wanted to be a man.

Mr. Linton had about three hundred acres of land and raised a few cows. He and his wife lived like paupers, but when they died they had a million dollars saved up. They just never spent money on anything—saved it all. What they needed, they grew themselves or got from their brown Jersey milk cow, Buttermilk.

They were old-style farmers—the last of an era. I was fortunate to know them for the last ten or fifteen years of their life. They milked Buttermilk every day, and since I was often there running around on the farm, Mr. Linton showed me how to milk her too. Mrs. Linton used some of the milk to make her own butter. I just thought that was normal—although on our farm, we didn't milk cows for ourselves. Our cattle were for beef.

He had a mule named Gray. I can remember walking along with Mr. Linton and plowing the garden with a hand plow pulled by old Gray. I look back on that now and think, *How remarkable is it that I got to plow a garden with a mule?* At the time, of course, I didn't think it was unusual. It was just what I did with Mr. Linton.

Mrs. Linton put up all her own food from their massive garden. They had a cellar where they stored it all. She even ground corn into cornmeal to make cornbread. Pretty much the only thing they didn't make on their own was sugar. For that, they had to go into town.

Mr. Linton died when I was nineteen years old. The contribution he made to my life is immeasurable. In a sense, he gave me a dual life—on one hand, I was a member of a fairly well-off family (although I never thought of it that way as a child) that owned a successful business and a farm; on the other, I was plowing a garden with a mule, milking a cow by hand, and cutting hay with a sickle-bar clipper. Mr. Linton was also a deeply spiritual man, and he told me on more than one occasion that knowing God was, as he would put it, "the most important thing in all the world." That has a profound impact on a little boy who looks up to a man as much as I looked up to Mr. Linton.

In fact when I was a boy, all of the influential men in my life—my dad, my grandpa, and Mr. Linton—were spiritual men, active in their churches. Even though my grandpa died when I was six and I have few memories of him, one stands out. My grandparents attended the South Harpeth Church of Christ. Congregational singing is unaccompanied in that denomination, and I remember standing next to my grandfather one Sunday morning, watching and hearing him sing, acapella, "How Great Thou Art." The fact that I remember that scene fifty-two years later implies that at some level, the boy I was recognized that something important was happening at that moment—something that was a part of the identity of my grandfather and, actually, my whole family.

When Mr. Linton died, his wife Mary Lou, who had never learned to drive, rode in the car with us to the funeral and then to the graveside—which was on our little family plot right on the farm. And then we dropped her off at her house, and, after we'd changed clothes, my dad and I got in the truck and headed down to the barn to feed the cattle. It was evening by that time, and dark. We drove past her house, and she was out on the porch feeding the dogs and tending to the other animals. I watched her moving through the yard and realized that this was the first time in many decades she'd done this in the evening without Mr. Linton. *Man, I'll bet she's sad about that,* I thought.

My dad, watching her as he drove, said "This is when it really gets hard."

The truth, I would learn later, is that it's all hard.

A big part of my summers growing up was showing calves at fairs, Hereford cattle shows, and 4-H shows across the region. Each kid in my family would have a calf. Every morning, we had to feed our calves and clean the stalls. When showtime came, we'd load them up in trucks and ride to the fairgrounds. The state 4-H Youth Livestock Exposition at the state fairgrounds in Nashville was one of the most thrilling weeks of my life—every year.

But of course before you could show the calves, you had to break them. These weren't tame calves raised in a farmyard like a pet. Our calves lived in pastures with lots of other cattle, and they were more than half wild.

Each year the five of us went out into the pasture and drove a group of cattle that had our chosen calves in it into a corral. You work cows by funneling them into progressively smaller spots. Our pastures are set up so that the pasture leads into a smaller pen which leads into a corral which funnels into a chute, which leads to a headgate.

There you would put its first halter on the calf. The halter had a rope lead about three feet long. When you show calves, they wear a halter with a lead rope so that you can walk them around within a show ring, so they need to get used to the halter. Once the halter is in place, you try to get them to someplace open where you can tie them up.

But these, remember, were wild cattle. And they would fight the halter all day long. So the first few days of breaking a calf can be harrowing. We would tie a long rope to the three-foot halter rope and we'd get three or four kids on the long rope, and then we'd release that calf from the headgate. It would be like releasing a bucking bronco out of a chute, and that calf would take the three or four of us holding onto the rope for a ride while we tried to pull it to the post where we intended to tie it up.

The youngest calves would be about 300 to 400 pounds. The oldest calves we showed would be 800 to 1,000 pounds. A calf that size at the other end of the rope will drag you a long way, given a chance. You break them in corrals so they can't drag you very far.

Eventually we would tie the short lead rope to a post, take the long rope off, and then get out of the way, because that calf would fight the rope for an hour, kicking and bucking.

Over the next several days, we would take the halter off and let those calves loose every night. And then catch them again the next morning and go through the same process again. And every day, there's a slight improvement in that calf's reaction. We would reward them with food for that improved reaction to being tied up, and slowly but surely they would allow us to touch them and brush them. But they fight each step.

So every year, the five of us kids would pick our calves and break them all at the same time. Over three or four weeks, we would train them to walk to our lead. We went through that every year, because we would show a different calf every year. That's because the calves age out of the process—you can only show them for about the first year and a half of their lives.

We didn't have cattle trailers to transport our calves to the fair. We just had trucks, generally a type of flatbed called a stake-bed truck that allowed you to insert stock gates in the sides and rear. My dad had a little makeshift roof that he put over the top of the truck bed where he would stack hay and feed to take to the show barn for the week. As astonishing as it now seems, we kids would sit up on the makeshift top and ride to the fairgrounds in Nashville. On top of a truck! Driving down the highway. My dad would be arrested for that these days.

My dad was always there whatever we kids were doing. As teenagers, of course, we did more and more of the work ourselves, but even when he didn't need to transport us and stay with us, he would want to know what class we were showing our calves in, and when. His office wasn't far from the fairgrounds. He'd drive over in his shirt and tie to watch us show our calves, then head back to work. He was a full-on kind of guy; he liked to be busy. He loved working on the farm and thought everybody should do it. He was very much an entrepreneur. He was the head of a national organization, Air Conditioning Contractors of America. He was the chairman of the board of elders of our church. He was a leader. But he was also very much a family man who was deeply committed to his wife and his family. He was not an absent father, ever.

For the whole week we slept at the fair, in the stalls. We would tie our calves outside—they slept better there than under the lights. Then we would clean their straw, sleep in their stall, and bring the calves back in in the morning. I loved the whole week—in the evenings, we would go to what they called the Fair Park and ride rides, then take care of our calves, sleep in their stalls, and show calves the next day. It was great.

They classified calves by ages. So the youngest calves would show first in the morning, gradually working up to the oldest calves. So we might be in class 2 and 9 and 18.

We didn't auction our cattle off after showing them, because we usually showed heifers. You generally only auction steers. So we would bring our heifer calves home.

My kids showed calves as well. A family tradition. My youngest, Sarah Kate, who's now a senior at Auburn University getting a degree in animal sciences, was the one who enjoyed it the most. She showed calves all the way through high school, and since her older siblings had all stopped showing calves by that time, those fairs and shows were often just the two of us, father and daughter, including some as far away as North Carolina.

Of my siblings, I was the one most involved in 4-H. I started in fourth grade. 4-H was about more than agriculture. Besides raising and showing livestock, I was doing public speaking and demonstrations. For your demonstration projects—mine were usually electrical projects because of my interest in engineering—4-H emphasized the records you kept. The solar energy project I did in 1977 won first place in the Tennessee high school electrical project category. That enabled me to go on to the National 4-H Congress in Chicago. For me, that was a big deal—not only because of the opportunity to compete at a national level, but because of the chance to visit Chicago. Our delegation was primarily a bunch of rural Tennessee kids who had, most of us, never been to the big city—*any* big city. We stayed at the Hilton Hotel near Lake Michigan and Michigan Avenue, the Miracle Mile, where such stores as Bloomingdale's and Saks Fifth Avenue could be found. For a kid from a farm on a dirt road in rural Tennessee, that was a memory I'll never forget—no matter how many big cities I've been to since.

Not all of my extended family lived on the farm. My mother was born and raised in downtown Memphis and went to Central High School. Her maiden name was Bartholomew. She and my grandparents attended Madison Heights Methodist Church as she was growing up. My grandfather worked for a well-known Memphis company, the John A. Denie Company.

I also had a set of cousins who lived in a typical middle-class neighborhood in an area of Memphis called Sherwood Forest. I thought of that set of cousins as my "city cousins." Every summer, they would come to stay with us for a couple of weeks—their chance to experience farm living. And my siblings and I would go stay with them in "the city" for a couple of weeks as well (and with my grandparents on Adams Avenue for part of that time).

I loved going to Memphis—they had so many things we didn't have on our little rural dirt road. A Popsicle truck made the rounds on their street. You could walk to the store. You played ball in the street with neighborhood kids—there were about ten kids, built-in playmates, living right there on the same street. You could ride your bikes so many different places and play in the storm drains that went under the streets. There were lights and people. I remember lying in bed at my grand-mother's house at night and hearing things we never heard at our house: sirens and traffic. At our house, if we heard any-thing at night, it was likely chirping tree frogs.

From my mom's side of the family, I also had cousins in Virginia and in Chattanooga. Every summer of my childhood we had a big family reunion weekend at our farm, and every-one on the Bartholomew side of the family came. Great fun. Everyone slept in tents on sleeping bags—twenty kids and eight adults. Then as people got married and there were more and more kids, it grew to forty, then fifty, then sixty people. That tradition continued for perhaps thirty years. We had the next-to-last family reunion two weeks before Carol Ann's accident.

Our farm sat in a hardworking rural area of the county, and that's where I grew up. Much has changed since then, and the community today has a much more diverse economy, but in those days our neighbors were mostly farmers. The students at Fairview Elementary where I went to school were mostly from farming or lower- and middle-class families. No, I didn't grow up poor, but we certainly weren't wealthy. In fact, we laugh now remembering how frugal my mother was, and still is. We would drive for an hour to go to the Utopia Shoe Store, a discount shoe store, once a year so that each kid could have a new pair of shoes. And we generally had only two pair—a pair of tennis shoes and a pair of "hard" shoes, as we called them, for church.

And I'm glad my siblings and I grew up that way. People are people, regardless of their job or how much money they make.

When I was a kid, I knew everybody who lived on every road around our farm. I rode my bicycle up and down all those roads. My two best friends in my grade were the only two guys who lived anywhere near me at all. Darwin was my best buddy and he lived about two miles from my house on the main road—which wasn't paved but was tarred and graveled. That was virtually next door. And Jody lived five or six miles from here. I would ride my bike to Darwin's house, and the two of us would ride to Jody's house. We'd put twenty miles a day on those old bikes.

Gone all day and nobody would have the slightest idea where we were or what we were doing. Hard to imagine that now. Except at our place. Our farm is on a dead-end road. There are only three or four more houses past mine, and the road ends at the last one. Nearly all of the houses on this three-mile road are occupied by family members. So even now it's still pretty safe here to let your kids roam.

When I was in first grade, there was one black child in my entire elementary school. She lived in an old log structure, kind of run-down, only about a half mile from our house. She was one of my friends. We sat together on the bus. One day somebody said something mean about her on the bus, and I got into a fight with him. Which led to me being kicked off the bus for a while; my mom had to drive me to school. But once I'd told her the story, she said that was okay because skin color shouldn't matter, and because in our family we stand up for our friends.

One day that girl didn't come to school anymore. It wasn't until later that I learned it was because someone had driven by their house and thrown a stick of dynamite at it. So the only black family that lived anywhere around here left.

It wasn't until years later, when I attended a junior-high school across the county, that I would ride the bus with a person of color again. I knew because of my upbringing that people were people regardless of wealth or skin color, but attending a recently desegregated school in the 1970s would open my eyes to just how deep seated the divisions that exist in society had become.

CHAPTER 3

Brace Yourself Like a Man

On the way to Vanderbilt University Medical Center, I called Carol Ann's parents in Birmingham. Her dad answered. "Charlie," I said, "something terrible has happened. Carol Ann's been in a really bad accident. You need to pack your bags and come up. Right now."

"It's that serious?"

I opened my mouth to respond, then hesitated. This was the worst thing to ever have to tell someone. His life was never going to be the same. But I had no choice. "Charlie, I don't think she's going to make it."

When I walked into the emergency room and told them who I was, the nurse said, "There's someone on the phone for you."

I said, "I can't talk on the phone." I felt more fragile than I had ever felt, as if it took all my concentration simply to hold my body together, to keep it from flying into a million pieces. I didn't have the emotional bandwidth to handle anyone else's fragility.

And the nurse said, "It's a family member."

I took the phone. It was Carol Ann's sister, the one we'd been on vacation with at Yellowstone just a couple of weeks before. "Bill, is it true?" she said. "What happened?"

And I said, "Elaine, Carol Ann isn't going to make it." I hadn't even talked to the doctor yet, but somehow I knew that was true.

Elaine began to weep. I knew she needed me to walk with her through this, but it was too much. I said, "I can't talk to you right now, Elaine. I'll talk to you when I know more."

As soon as I turned away from the phone, a doctor approached, introduced himself as the one treating Carol Ann, and motioned toward a small private room off to the side. There we stood as he explained Carol Ann's condition in medical terms that went right over my head. Then he summed it up: "Barring a miracle, she will not live." I couldn't respond. I didn't know what to do, what I should feel, what I should say. It was like when I was a kid and my grandfather died, and I had to watch my older siblings for a clue how to act. Now, I needed some hint as to how people respond when their entire lives are blown apart.

The door to the small room opened and one of my best friends, a cardiologist, entered. He explained everything in layman's terms, and as he did, my fear grew. "Dick," I said, "is she going to hang on like this forever?" The thought of someone so vibrant, so full of life, reduced to such a life was horrible.

"No," Dick said, "she won't live long. It will be very brief."

"She's in a coma," the other doctor added. "I should tell you this: There's no way we can know for sure, but there's a good possibility that she can hear and understand, even in a coma."

Was this true? Or was it something they tell grieving family members when their loved ones are dying? I didn't know, and I was too numb to question it.

"On the chance that she can hear you," he said, "I encourage you to speak to her. She won't hang on long."

Then I went alone into her room, in disbelief and shock, and closed the door. I seemed to be experiencing everything from a great distance, as if I had been anesthetized—but that didn't make it any less painful. Tubes for oxygen had been hung over her ears and into her nose. She had something wrapped around her head—it may have been a gauze bandage, but I envision it like a bandanna. It covered the worst of her injuries. Her face looked uninjured. As if she were asleep.

The doctor had encouraged me to speak to her. But what do you say to the one whose life is more dear to you than your own, the one with whom you have become one flesh, when she's lying there dying? When you're not sure it even makes sense to believe that she can hear you? When life as you know it has ended?

And then I remembered the passage from Job that Carol Ann had read to me on our Yellowstone trip just two weeks before, at a time when we were amazed at how beautifully our lives were unfolding. I remembered that I'd been convinced then that God was attempting to speak to me through that passage. Had he been preparing me for this moment?

There was a Bible in the room. I opened it, found the passage in Job 39 and 40, and began reading it aloud to her.

> "'Who is this that obscures my plans
>   with words without knowledge?
> Brace yourself like a man …'"

I couldn't read any further. I choked. But not simply because of my grief. As soon as I'd read the first few words, it was as if reading them had opened the door and God was speaking to me. *I'm the same today, on the worst day of your life,* he said, *as I was two weeks ago on the best day of your life. I haven't changed. Your circumstances have changed, but I haven't. Everything you and Carol Ann talked about and rejoiced about in that beautiful place I created for you to enjoy is true. Now is not the time to shake your fist at me and try to figure this all out.*

That all came to me in far less time than it just took you to read it. And it was a real gift for me. I walked out of that hospital room knowing that despite the fact that my life had just been turned upside down, I was not alone in this. That was a very powerful reality. Was it a comfort? No—there was no comforting me at that moment. But it allowed me to walk out understanding that there was more to this than I could see.

It's a very weird feeling knowing that you've been prepared by God for something. Bringing that passage in Job to Carol Ann's mind during our Yellowstone trip was only one of the ways God had prepared us for the incredible difficulty of losing her. After all, is it not the whole point of the passage that God is all-powerful and completely in control, and that his might and his wisdom surpass ours in every conceivable way, and that he has been that way for eons beyond counting before I was even born? Even the words: "Brace yourself..."

He prepared us in other ways as well.

Our church held a conference about a week before her accident. We attended on a Saturday. At one point, conferees were asked—after a lead-in about how we don't take the time to express to our spouses how much they mean to us—to take ten minutes, just you and your spouse, to tell your spouse what you would like them to know that you don't tell them.

So there Carol Ann and I sat, on the Saturday before her accident, and told each other all of the things we wanted to say. I don't remember exactly what I said to her, but I do know that I had the chance to tell her what I'd always known I should say—and to hear the same from her. You would have a hard time convincing me that God didn't know exactly what was coming and was preparing us for it. *Brace yourself...*

That following Monday, about four couples from church came for dinner on our back porch. We laughed and talked about our kids. Carol Ann joked about being a helicopter mom. It was a delightful time with some of our best friends.

The next morning I was sitting where I always sit to read in the morning—on a couch near the stone fireplace in our large family room, where I can look out across our pastures—when Carol Ann came downstairs. When someone dies, it's amazing how much you remember about the very last everything you experienced with them. I remember her coming into the room that morning, and I asked her about a particular passage of Scripture I'd been reading: "What do you think this means?" And we talked for a few minutes about that passage. Then I headed off to work.

The next time I saw her, she was riding horseback across the river with Sarah Kate on the saddle in front of her.

Carol Ann was well known and well loved in Franklin and Nashville, and about an hour after her Life Flight helicopter arrived at Vanderbilt University Medical Center, I walked from her room out into the waiting room and there were a hundred people there. It grew to two hundred, then three hundred. The only problem: I'm not a person who seeks out others when I'm in pain. I tend to retreat. So I didn't want to see any of the people gathered there. They were dear friends, not just of Carol Ann's but of mine, but I turned around and walked back down the hall. *I can't do this. I can't do it,* I thought. So I didn't.

So began an extremely long and incredibly beautiful but horrible experience: three days in the hospital awaiting what we all knew was coming, with hundreds of people there twenty-four hours a day. Many of them wanted to see me, but I didn't want to see anybody other than four or five friends I was very close to—their presence, because of our closeness, was less painful to me.

Our eldest child, Jessica, fourteen at the time, was in Mexico on a missions trip with our church youth group. Carol Ann and I had driven her down to the church to join the group and depart just a couple of days before. But now, of course, she would have to come home, and immediately. Michael W. Smith, the musician and composer, was and is a good friend and attended our church, and he sent his private jet to go get her in Mexico, with my dad on board so that Jessica wouldn't have to fly back all alone.

After the misery of the hospital, I went home about midnight. Mom was still there: she'd been waiting while the kids slept. I waited up for Jessica to get home. Dad hadn't told her about Carol Ann. He and I both believed that I should be the one to do that, but she had already guessed that Mom must be dead or dying—she just didn't know the details. When she walked in the front door, I took her in my arms and told her that her mom had been in a terrible accident and that she was going to die. And she wailed.

I asked my mom and dad to leave, to give the kids and me time alone.

Because we'd just had a family reunion on the farm the week before (one more way God had prepared us for this day), we'd had to move some beds around, and Carol Ann and I had been sleeping on just a mattress on the floor in our bedroom. Jessica and I went upstairs and sat on that mattress, and she cried so loudly that she woke the boys. First they came in, and then Sarah Kate. We all lay on that mattress on the floor all night long. I would say that we slept there, except that none of us slept for very long. We cried and talked and cried and talked. They had all already heard me say that Mom was going to die, but now I told them something else very important: I told them that we would survive—that life would go on. We would have to do it without my wife and their mother, but we would do it.

About 4:00 in the morning, I thought everyone was asleep. Then I heard Caleb say, "Dad? I don't think I'm going to make it."

I said, "Come here, son."

He scooted over beside me.

I said, "What do you mean?"

He said, "I'm really scared."

In addition to fears that nearly all kids share—such as losing their parents—all kids have fears that are peculiar to them. One of Caleb's personalized fears was that he was afraid of being in the woods—to the extent that other boys sometimes teased him about it. He feared the woods because he thought there were cougars there.

That night, he said, "I'm afraid. It feels like I'm in the woods. And it's dark. And I'm alone."

I said, "Caleb, I feel kind of like that too. But you're not alone. It's really dark and you can't see—that much is true. I'm right beside you. I can't see, either, but I think Jesus is right beside me. And I'm sure he knows where he is. And if we just stand here for a little while, it will get light again. And then we'll see where we are."

Then he went to sleep.

We awoke the next day to a nightmare life.

Going to the hospital.

Thousands of people—most of them very sweet and well known to us.

Talking to doctors.

Coming home.

Going back to the hospital.

Then home again.

Lots of prayers—many of them powerful prayers from people who were hoping and believing for healing for Carol Ann.

Meals.

Flowers.

Phone calls.

An overwhelming outpouring of love and goodwill.

Twenty-four-hour prayer vigils.

The chapel at the hospital packed all the time.

After three days of that, the doctor said, "I know this is a question no one wants to face about a loved one, but Carol Ann's brain hasn't functioned since her admission to the hospital, and there's no chance that it's ever going to. How long should we leave her on life support?"

That was a decision I'd never had to make before, and I needed help. I talked to my pastor, I talked to my kids, and in the end I decided that what Carol Ann would want when her physical body had run its course is for us to turn the oxygen off. We did.

But her body hung on—in fact, she was still breathing that night when too tired to stay awake any longer, I went home. Even that decision to go home seemed more than I could handle in the midst of the heartbreak and chaos.

A nurse called me the next morning and said, "You need to get over here." I had taken all my kids in to see her the day before. Each one of them got to go in and have their own time alone with her, except for Sarah Kate—I thought she was too young, but now I think that was a bad call. So I drove over there as fast as I could and rushed in. Carol Ann's three sisters were there—they'd been there all three days. But now I asked them, and everybody else, to let us have this time alone. I allowed no one to stay but my pastor, Don Finto.

I leaned in close to her and said, "Carol Ann—it's okay. I'm here. The kids are okay, and they'll continue to be okay, because I'm going to take care of them. I love you. I will miss you every day. But it's okay. You can go." And she took one deep breath and was gone. Just like that. I hadn't been there five minutes.

I can't describe it. It was almost as if her chains had been released and she was set free. It was a moment I had dreaded, but when it came, it wasn't dreadful at all. It was bitter, yes—very bitter—but there was a thread of sweetness too.

I walked down to the waiting room, which was still filled to overflowing. I gave a few hugs, told everyone, "She's gone," and then I walked out. I got in my car and drove home. Jessica was there and some friends were with her, so I decided she was all right. I took Jacob and Caleb together up to a favorite spot on the farm, where we lay down on our backs and talked. "Hey, y'all," I said. "You know what your mom is probably doing right now? I'm guessing she's being introduced to John the disciple and I don't know who all, Abraham maybe." We talked for a while about what she might be doing in heaven.

And that was important. Because otherwise, the kids might get the idea that she's nowhere. *My mom has always been here, but she's not here now. So she's not anywhere.* But she is.

We lay there and talked for an hour. I tried to be as reassuring as I could be. Then I took them back to my mom's house, which, by this time, was filled with people.

Then it was Sarah Kate's turn. She and I went for a four-wheeler ride, one of her favorite things. Then we got off and walked. "This place was one of your mom's favorite spots, did you know that?" I said. "And maybe it still is. But your mom went to heaven today. So we won't get to see her for a while." I was trying to be truthful and yet not too frightening at the same time.

Then Sarah Kate amazed me. "You know what, Dad?" she said. "Mom's holding my hand."

"She is?"

And she said, "Yeah. Right now."

We walked along in silence for a while—I didn't know what to say to that. And then she said, "She just let go."

CHAPTER 4

COURTING
CAROL ANN

Until my older sister Cynthia got a basketball scholarship to Auburn University, I never knew what or where Auburn was. But after I'd visited her there, I thought, *I love this place—this is where I want to go to college.* Before that, I'd been planning to go to Vanderbilt—another great university— and in fact I'd already been accepted there. But Vanderbilt is in Nashville, just down the road, and like recent high-school graduates everywhere and in every generation, I thought, *It would be so much more fun to go away to school.*

At one of our functions my junior year, one of my fraternity brothers brought a girl I thought was particularly beautiful. Her name was Carol Ann. We met that night, but after all she was there with somebody else. And I was dating someone else, too—someone, in fact, who lived in Carol Ann's dorm. I would go over there often to pick up my girlfriend or to just hang out—they had a lobby with a TV. Guys weren't allowed up in the girls' rooms, but the girls could come down and sit with their dates or guy friends in the lobby.

Carol Ann lived across the hall from the girl I was dating. I kept running into her in the lobby and elsewhere, and I was definitely interested.

I was in engineering school, and back in those days that meant that most of my classmates were men. I took a home economics course (Clothing and Man) as an elective so that I would have at least one class with girls in it. My goal was simple: I wasn't dating anybody when I signed up for the class, and I just wanted to meet some girls. The girl who sat next to me in the class was Corinne, a member of the sorority Carol Ann had joined.

By that time I'd broken up with the girl I'd been dating. So I asked Corinne, "There's a girl in your sorority I want to go out with. Can you find out if she has a boyfriend?"

Corinne set us up, and we had a blind date. Or only semi-blind, since I knew who she was—I don't think she remembered me from the party. And I came home from that date to the house where I lived with seven guys. They were all sitting around watching TV. I came in late, midnight or so, and plopped down and said, "I just went out with the girl I'm going to marry."

They laughed. "After just one date? Who is it?" they asked.

"Carol Ann Person."

I was completely smitten. At least *I* was. Carol Ann, not so much.

That was in early November. I asked her if I could come to Birmingham, her home, over the Christmas break to see her and meet her parents. When she said yes, I was excited— this must mean she was serious. I had great expectations for how wonderful that visit was going to be, until I got there and she told me that she had a boyfriend, Loren, who lived in Oregon. She had met him working in Yellowstone the summer before. "We've been dating for a couple of months and you're just now getting around to telling me about Loren?" I said, frustrated.

We didn't stop dating. There was just always a big question about this second guy out in Oregon. And the question got even bigger at spring break, when he came out to go camping with her and her family—something that, I now learned, they had planned way back in the fall. As big a crush as I had on her, I'd had about enough. "At the end of spring break," I told her, "you need to decide. If it's him, okay. But at least I'll know where I stand. I don't want to keep seeing you if you have another boyfriend."

"It's all over with Loren," she told me after the camping trip.

That was near the end of our junior year. We dated all through our senior year, but the challenges appeared right away. For one thing, she said, "I never want to get married. If you're dating me because you think we might get married, then you need to know that won't happen." She was a free spirit—besides working in Yellowstone, she'd backpacked all over and was independent and fearless.

Not a problem for me—I loved challenges. *You won't get married?* I thought. *Oh, yeah, you will.*

I wooed her all through that school year. And talked her into it—we got engaged in June, right after graduation. She was very much a prize for me. She was beautiful, of course, but also popular and smart. She had it all—a far more wonderful woman than I'd ever thought I could win.

We planned to be married in September.

At least that was the *plan.*

Every engagement has issues. One of ours was my huge, interconnected family. I was very close to my parents, and I spent a lot of time on the farm. All the time we were dating, it was all about coming back out to the farm, coming to my parents' for Sunday lunch, and so on. It scared her. Something that had been a strength, a treasure, all my life now became, to Carol Ann at least, a threat. "Is your family more important?" she would ask. "Are you going to be able to separate yourself from them enough that we can have a life of our own?" And she had a legitimate concern. The first real fights we had were when she would say, "I don't *want* to go out to the farm today." Remember, she was independent and strong-willed—she didn't like being poured into someone else's mold.

Her fears that I was too close to my family made me mad. Even if she was right, it still made me mad. I thought my relationship with my family was a rare and beautiful thing—how could she resist it?

What if I'm making a big mistake? I wondered. *What if I'm about to marry somebody who's going to make my life worse, not better, and what if I make her life worse as well?* I got a terrible case of cold feet. I was in turmoil. And the closer the wedding date came, the worse it got. For me, and also for Carol Ann.

Then something really strange happened. I had a dream that I was in church—not our church, and not any church I actually knew, but a little church on a hillside. And I looked out the window and could see her coming, across the open pastures of our farm. She had on a wedding dress. And I knew it was our wedding day, and we were about to get married. And I couldn't get out of the church—I couldn't get away. I was locked in. It was like being in jail—I couldn't get out. Meanwhile, she was coming closer ... and closer....

I woke up and tried to make sense of the dream. I had been praying for guidance about whether to get married. Maybe God was trying to tell me something. Maybe—in fact, almost certainly—he'd sent the dream as an answer to my prayers. *I can't go through with it,* I thought. *I can't do that to Carol Ann, and I can't do it to myself.*

I don't remember all of the details of the big argument we got into a few days after I had that dream. I do remember, though, that it was Carol Ann who first said, "We don't need to go through with this. We can call it off."

So we called it off. Six weeks before our wedding date. We had the wedding invitations, all the plans were made—everything.

If you think that would be traumatic, you're right. Yes, I had major cold feet, but we were about to get *married,* for Pete's sake. It was more than just breaking up with a girlfriend. I remember crying. I didn't have a sense of relief. I had a sense of great loss. I really loved her.

My dad said, "You just want what you can't get. When you get it, then you don't want it. You know what your problem is? You like the battle. You like the challenge. When you first met Carol Ann, she had a boyfriend. That made her a challenge. Then she said she wouldn't marry you. Another challenge. Now you're about to get married—and you don't want her anymore." But as much truth as there was in what he said, it was also true that I desperately loved her and was devastated that I'd lost her.

To make things harder, Carol Ann was living in Nashville by that time. She had moved here before we got engaged—she was an artist and had come here for a job, working at the publishing house of what was then called the Baptist Sunday School Board. We even went to the same church and had a lot of the same friends. I couldn't handle that—I switched to a different church.

I really believed, as I had told my roommates a couple of years earlier, that she was the person I was going to marry. And I was deeply in love with her. But the breakup was mostly my fault—I was immature. In the back of my mind, though, I always figured we'd get back together. It was just a matter of time.

Weeks went by. Months. A year. It wasn't happening.

My brother got married that next fall, and Carol Ann, who was a friend of my sister-in-law-to-be, took part in that wedding as a server. We hadn't seen each other for months, and I knew it would be awkward—but I was also eager to see her. I still believed that one day we'd get back together.

It was just as awkward as I'd feared it would be. Neither of us had much to say. I remember walking away thinking, *If that's how it's going to go, I'm glad we never got back together. I was wrong—I'm never going to marry her. In fact, since she's the best person I could ever hope to marry, maybe I'll just never get married. There'll never be anyone that good for me again.* It seems a bit silly now, but I was pretty serious about it at the time. I prayed, *Not my will, Lord, but yours. If you ever want me to get married, you're going to have to choose someone for me and bring her into my life, because I can't imagine it happening on my own.*

I stopped by Carol Ann's house a few months later at Christmas. No real ulterior motive. I just wanted to say merry

Christmas. After all, I'd once thought I was going to marry this girl—the least I could do is wish her a merry Christmas. So when she came to the door, I did. "And please tell your folks I said hey. I hope you have a great holiday."

She invited me in. We chatted, and then I said, "Well, I'd better go. I have to make a cake for our Christmas party. I told everybody I know how to make coconut cake, which of course was a big lie. But they believed me and asked me to make one, so now I have to go home and do it."

She laughed. "You have no idea how to do it, do you?"

I shook my head.

"Do you want me to help you?"

So we went to the store and bought the stuff and went back to my place and baked a coconut cake. And we had great fun doing it—almost like we'd never been apart.

When it was time for her to leave, I helped her into her coat and said, "When you get back from Christmas at your parents' house, let's go out again."

We got engaged in March—again. And married in June.

CHAPTER 5

Even the Air Feels Different

The time I spent with each of my kids on the last day of Carol Ann's life, reassuring them, started something: For a long time afterward, I would spend about an hour a day with each of my kids individually.

It was as much for my benefit as for theirs. I hadn't gone back to work and had no desire to, so I had extra time. Someone was fixing every meal. I was grief-stricken, mortified, horrified, and more alone than I had ever been. Every morning I would wake up and think, *How am I going to get through this day? What can I do to fill the interminable hours?*

One of the few constructive, purposeful things I could think of was that time with each kid. We talked a lot, and some of those conversations were incredible. Caleb in particular, nine years old, would say the most poignant things. I remember sitting on the front porch with him one day very soon after she died—it was still July. In Tennessee as elsewhere, certain things in nature happen at particular times of the year, like the first buttercup you see in February or the first whippoorwill you hear in May. Starting in late July and then through August, especially when it's really hot outside in the middle of the day, the cicadas make a repetitive chirping sound: *chh, chh, chh.*

"You hear that sound?" Caleb asked as we sat on the porch.

I nodded. "I hear it."

He said, "I *used* to like that sound."

That was true for all of us. Living on the farm as close to nature as we are, there were so many reminders for the next few years of what had happened in July of 2000. The next year, and the next and the next, when one particular kind of wildflower started blooming, I would think, *It's coming.*

Jacob, during one of the times the two of us spent together, said, "Everything's different now."

"Yes, it is," I said.

And he said, "Even the air feels different."

I stopped walking, amazed. He was right—the air did feel different from when Carol Ann was alive.

Time has lessened that effect for all of us—mercifully. But in so many ways, in those first years, what had been sweet was now bitter.

I remember taking Caleb and Jacob to a Titans game weeks after the accident. Just to fill the hours. It was in August, so it was probably a preseason game. But even so, the stadium was full of people and everyone was cheering. I remember standing along with everyone else and thinking, *This is all wrong. These people shouldn't be happy.* On one level I knew that it was good for them to be happy, but emotionally I felt like, *Hey—my world just stopped. So everyone's world should be stopped.*

For years afterward, there were movies I just couldn't watch. I've walked out of theaters. Somebody gets shot. There's some fatal accident. Someone loses a spouse, or a young child loses a parent. And I would get up and walk out. I couldn't do it.

Until your heart is broken, you don't realize that it's all around you constantly.

Just before the funeral, we were all down in the basement family room together. We have a TV down there and a bunch of big soft overstuffed chairs. A good place to relax—but with one bittersweet quality: We had finished it just a month before Carol Ann's accident.

On that day before the funeral, one of the kids said, "We'll never go on vacation again, will we?" Of course—how could they conceive of a family vacation when the beating heart of the family wasn't beating anymore?

But I said, "We will, actually. Right now, I don't really *want* to go on vacation without your mom. But believe it or not, there will come a day when our life will start to seem kind of normal again. And I hate even saying that because, for now, I don't *want* it to feel normal without her. But one day we'll laugh again. Life will feel good again."

An idea struck me. "Wait a minute." I got up and grabbed a yardstick nearby and sat back down and held it up. "Pretend this yardstick is a timeline. It represents the passage of time." I touched one end. "Right here is where the earth started." I moved my finger a little. "And maybe this is where the flood was and Noah's Ark, and this is where Jesus was born. Maybe this is where America was discovered. And the Revolutionary war." I had their attention. "Right here is where your mom and I were born. You four kids were born here and here and here and here. And this—right here—this is where your mom died. She should have lived to here—" I scooted my finger a couple of inches down the stick—"but she didn't. She died back here." I paused a moment for that to sink in, then pointed to a new spot. "This is about where I'll probably live to. The four of you will probably live a whole lot longer than that, so you'll probably live to about here. And after that, then we go to heaven. And how long does heaven last? Clear down to here—" I slid my finger to the end of the stick—"and then it goes across the rug and it goes out the window and down the driveway and out to the Interstate where we went in the RV. And it goes all the way out across Nebraska and Wyoming. Remember, all of us will be together in heaven all this time, all of us including

Mom. And from Wyoming it goes up to Beartooth Pass and then shoots up to the stars, and then you can't see how long it goes. But it just keeps going."

Then I held up the stick again and marked off the distance from Carol Ann's death to the time we're all reunited in heaven. "We just have to go from here to here without her." I swept my hand from the stick toward the window. "And then we'll be together with her for all that." I looked at my kids. "We can do this. We'll have to help each other out. And God will help us too." I handed the stick to Jessica, and they passed it around. "It may seem like a long time, but it's really not. We can do this."

That little talk changed the nature of our conversation about missing Carol Ann. Sometimes, especially with Sarah Kate, I would say, "When are we going to see Mom?"

And she'd say, "In just a few minutes."

Another time, Caleb said, "I don't think what everybody says about heaven is true."

"What do you mean?" I said.

"They say there's no tears in heaven. But that would mean Mom is in heaven watching all of us down here crying and sad and brokenhearted, and it doesn't make her sad. I don't believe that."

I had to think before I responded. Finally, I said, "Caleb, I think it's kind of like Christmas morning in our house."

I should explain that at our house, we had our own peculiar but much-beloved Christmas madhouse. We didn't wrap gifts at Christmas. The kids went to bed, and we stayed up putting everything out. Unwrapped. But we put it in four different places. Each of the kids had a chair or a spot that was theirs, and believe me they knew exactly which spot was theirs. So when they started down the stairs on Christmas morning, they had to stay up near the top until I gave the count: "One, two, three, go!" Then they all stampeded in to their own spot and their own pile of unwrapped gifts. Everything happened at once. As I say, it was a madhouse, but we wouldn't have had it any other way.

The year Carol Ann passed away, Caleb was nine and he had been wanting a go-cart and was saving his money up to buy one. So I said, "I think it will be like Christmas morning, Caleb. Except that when you come running in and Jessica is looking at all her stuff, and Sarah Kate's gifts are up on the sofa and she's digging through them, and Jacob too—there's nothing in *your* chair. And there you stand, sad and crying, thinking that we forgot you or we don't love you. It would be terrible!

"And to make it worse, standing over in the doorway to the kitchen is Mom, and she's got the biggest smile on her face you've ever seen. That makes you feel even worse, because you think, *Why is she so happy? Doesn't she love me? Doesn't she see I've got nothing for Christmas? How can she be so happy when I'm so sad?* What you can't see, though, is that behind her, where you can't see it, is the coolest, biggest go-cart you can imagine. It was too big to put in the living room, but we managed to get it into the kitchen. It's got four-wheel drive, a roll bar, everything. You're looking at that empty chair and crying. But your mom is laughing, not because she's mocking you but because she knows that in just a minute you'll walk into the kitchen and have the best Christmas you'll ever have.

"I don't know what heaven will be like, Caleb—but I think it will be something like that."

CHAPTER 6

FIVE MINUTES
TOO LATE

Every life contains moments when you realize you've accomplished a significant milestone, perhaps a loss and perhaps an accomplishment—a moment either long sought or long dreaded after which your life will proceed in a different direction. One such moment, in a negative sense, was when I raced up that grassy hill behind our barn and found Carol Ann bleeding, unconscious, and dying on the rocky ground. Another, far more positive, was the day we brought them home from the hospital, when I stood looking down at a bassinet that contained our two healthy newborn twin boys, Jacob and Caleb.

They were born five years after our daughter Jessica. That was not because we made a conscious decision to allow five years between kids. We had, in fact, made many attempts to have a child in those intervening years. Carol Ann had gotten pregnant five times between Jessica and the twins. None of those pregnancies had resulted in a healthy birth. As I stood and looked down at my two new sons, it all came rushing back to me—all of the struggle, the trauma, and the pain and tears and hopelessness of trying again and again for five years after Jessica—and now those desperate hopes had come to fruition in these two boys. The pain was behind us now, and I was overcome with appreciation and an incredible sense of redemption.

It's a pattern that God has woven into my life time and time again. The bitter with the sweet.

When Carol Ann and I married, I'd been living in a little house in downtown Franklin, maybe a thousand square feet, that I'd bought when I got out of school. I think I paid $35,000 for that house—it's probably worth ten times that now.

We lived there at first. Carol Ann was working at the Sunday School Board, I worked at our family business, and everything was great. We were overjoyed when she got pregnant, but it turned out to be an ectopic pregnancy—a tubal pregnancy. That was hard for a couple who hadn't been married long and were still getting used to being husband and wife, but we were young and resilient.

We both left for work at the same time in the mornings, and one morning a few months later I walked out the back door to get into the car with Carol Ann right behind me. But by the time I'd opened her car door, she was nowhere in sight. Where'd she go? I walked back into the house and found her in the bathroom, sick and vomiting.

She obviously felt miserable, but I smiled anyway. "You're pregnant again, aren't you?" I said.

We were both excited about the pregnancy, but apprehensive at the same time because of the ectopic pregnancy we'd just been through. And our apprehension only increased when Carol Ann had a positive alpha-fetoprotein test—a marker for genetic abnormalities such as spina bifida. You can take the test again to guard against false positives, which aren't unusual, but you have to wait several days before you can retake it, and those were very difficult days for us. Carol Ann cried a lot. But despite our disappointment and our apprehension about the health of our unborn child, we both knew what we would do: "If the baby has a defect," we said, "then it does. There would be no better parents than us for a kid with a birth defect." Not that we really had any idea what challenges or difficulties life with a disabled child would entail—but we did know that we had no intention of terminating the pregnancy regardless of what birth defects our child might have. We were not, nor am I now, in favor of abortion. We both agreed that if God sent special challenges into our lives, then he would use them.

We had no idea how many times in our lives we would be forced to fall back—and *fall* is the right word—on that same belief, or how exhausted we would be when we did so.

The second test was negative. False alarm. And our long-awaited, healthy baby girl Jessica was born, and life was great. Everything, we felt, was as it should be.

Carol Ann had an Uncle John who had never married and had no children. When he died, the family discovered that he'd been saving money all his life. There were plenty of relatives to share in the million dollars or so that he left. Carol Ann got about $20,000, and that seemed like a fortune to us then. It was enough for us to begin building a house for ourselves on one of my favorite areas of the farm; we financed the rest. I still live in the same place in a larger version of that house—I just added on to it over time. We had Jessica's one-year birthday on the front porch of the new house.

We wanted more than one child, and Carol Ann got pregnant again. We were more hopeful for a successful pregnancy now that we'd been through one. Even so, she miscarried. And that was hard on us both, but especially Carol Ann. The doctor advised us to wait a few months before trying again. When we did, she got pregnant again right away—and had another miscarriage.

Carol Ann's miscarriages weren't early in the pregnancy. One came at eleven or twelve weeks, and one of them at about fifteen weeks, after we'd already heard the heartbeat. The first one was really difficult. But after the second one, we really started to question things. Were we drastically flawed physically so that we would never have another live baby? We wanted to have kids close together, and Jessica was already almost three by the time we'd lost the second one.

When Carol Ann got pregnant the next time we held our breath, unsure every minute whether something would go wrong. But as the weeks passed, the baby seemed fine, Carol Ann was fine—maybe this time, everything would work out. Life was good!

Carol Ann was able to carry the baby full term. She began having contractions one night, and the next morning we decided that even though the contractions were irregular and we doubted that she was fully in labor, she and her mother (who had come to stay with us in anticipation of the baby coming) would go to the hospital to have it checked out. Meanwhile, I would stop by the office to pick up some paperwork for the next few days, figuring that if she was in labor, I would spend some time at home with Carol Ann and the baby. "Call me when you get there and they examine you," I said, "so I'll know whether I need to drop everything and head over there." I didn't expect that I would—judging from how things had gone with Jessica's birth, I expected this to be an all-day affair.

I expected a call from Carol Ann or her mom soon after I arrived at the office, if only to let me know how things were going. But as I sat there sorting through paperwork and correspondence and leaving notes for those who'd be covering for me while I was gone, she didn't call. And didn't call. I wondered what was taking so long—perhaps she hadn't been in labor after all.

Then her doctor, who was a friend, called. That wasn't a good sign. The first words I said were, "There's something wrong."

"You need to get here right away," he said.

"Has our baby died?"

He said, "We think so."

I hung up and walked into my dad's office—he was still working there as an important part of Lee Company. He looked up as soon as I walked in, and his face registered shock, so I know that my grief was showing. I said, "Dad, our baby died," and started to cry.

He reacted in stunned disbelief. He hugged me and said, "I'm coming with you."

"No, don't come," I said. "I need to go by myself."

When Carol Ann had checked into the hospital, the baby had seemed to be doing fine.

"That is one active baby," the nurse chuckled as she strapped on a monitor to check the heartbeat. But once the monitor was in place, she couldn't find a heartbeat. "There must be something wrong with this monitor," the nurse said. She took it off, rolled it away, and called for another monitor.

Still no heartbeat.

In that five minutes between the time Carol Ann and the nurse were remarking on how active the baby was and the time they couldn't find a heartbeat, the baby had died. There was a problem with the umbilical cord—a problem that could have been corrected if it had been detected just minutes earlier. The reason the baby had been so active was because it had been in distress.

For a young couple eager for their next baby and relieved, after two miscarriages, to bring a baby to full term, it was devastating. To go through all of that, and then be just five minutes too late.

It was horrible. The entire day was a traumatic, terrible experience. Since the baby was already dead, the doctors gave Carol Ann Pitocin, a drug that induces labor.

And then there she was, our daughter. Cynthia Kate. A perfectly formed little girl. We kept her with us for about an hour. My parents came in. Carol Ann's parents came in. Our pastor came. And then they took her and she was gone.

I've talked in this book about the bittersweet nature of life. There was nothing sweet about that day or anything connected with it. It was really bitter and really hard. I stayed alongside Carol Ann in the hospital bed all that night. Being in the maternity ward, we could hear babies crying in the nursery. But ours wasn't. And we were utterly miserable.

The next day we emptied out our hospital room of all of the things we had brought to bring the baby home in. Clothes. An infant car seat. We packed it all up and carried it out to the car and loaded it up. But there was one thing missing. No baby.

We got into the car and drove away. Just the two of us. It was the most empty and terrible feeling. Desolate.

And then we came home to an empty nursery. And to Jessica, who wanted to know where her baby sister was. It was total misery. Carol Ann cried nonstop.

We both struggled, but it hit Carol Ann particularly hard—to the extent that I wondered how and when she would be able to crawl out of it. It's not something you ever get over. You get through it, you get past it—but you don't get over it.

Three or four weeks after losing Cynthia Kate, on a hot May morning, Carol Ann and I were having coffee on the front porch. Jessica had spent the night at my parents' house, so it was just the two of us. Carol Ann cried frequently that morning, as she'd been doing ever since we'd lost the baby.

Even though she was still in her nightgown, she got up and went for a walk down the driveway. To some, I'm sure it sounds bizarre to wander down your driveway in nothing but your nightgown—but remember that we lived on a farm, screened by trees, and had a very long driveway.

All the flowers were up, and the grass was green. I had already mowed it once that year. Even though it was only May, it was beginning to feel like summer. But despite the warmth and the flowers, the hum of bees, the trees heavy with leaves, I remember thinking as I sat there that it would be a very empty summer for Carol Ann and me.

She must have been gone for close to an hour. And the whole time, I sat there drinking coffee and wondering, *Will she ever be the same? Will she be able to find a way to carry on and resume her roles as wife and mother? Or have Jessica and I lost her? Will she find a way to pick things up again with our friends and relatives? Or will she walk through life as she is now, sad and broken?*

Eventually I saw her slowly walking back up the driveway. As she came up the steps to the porch and sat back in her chair, I looked at her closely and thought, *I wonder what happened.*

Her whole demeanor has changed. But I couldn't tell exactly what her changed look meant. Was she calmer? More at peace? Determined? I was just about to ask her about it when she said, "God showed me I've been chosen."

Chosen? "I'm not sure what you mean," I said. "Chosen to suffer? Chosen for some task?"

And she said, "I don't know. He just let me know I was chosen."

We sat on the porch that day and discussed it. She couldn't be sure, but what Carol Ann felt God had been communicating is that he had chosen her to experience something most people don't—something difficult, something terrible, but something that God knew she was strong enough to handle. And through the growth she would experience as a result of that experience, she would be better able to comfort and assist others in their own hours of need.

That morning and its revelation started something in Carol Ann. It was a turning point, a milestone. From that hour on, almost as if a switch in her head had suddenly been flicked on, her perspective changed. She was able to see herself as a central player in a story God was writing—and that helped her to define for herself who she was: a remarkable woman who carried things deeply.

It didn't erase her grief about Cynthia Kate, but now she had an assurance that something good would come—that it wasn't senseless. That there was some purpose, reason, and value behind what we had gone through. Our circumstances hadn't suddenly changed while she walked down the driveway. We still had no baby in our arms. But even so, somehow a tragedy had gone from senseless to hopeful. The thread of hope that God has repeatedly woven through our lives, even at the moments when we least expected it or looked for it, was suddenly shining out again.

From that morning, she felt that she had a greater understanding of what her life was to be about. It was not really about her. It was about other people. From then on, Carol Ann lived her life thinking about others and how her life might impact them for good. She had always been a generous and compassionate woman, but after that walk down the driveway that day, she invested in other people's lives in rich, surprising ways.

She spent a lot of her life thereafter reaching out to others who were going through struggle. She was quick to make a phone call to someone in crisis, quick to drive across town and spend hours with someone struggling. I used to tease her gently and tell her that she must have a phone ministry, since she spent so much time on the phone talking to other women going through troubled times.

I confess—sometimes I felt jealous of her time. But after her death, I told someone, "I'm so glad that she lived her life not the way I wanted her to, but rather in the way she believed she should." Her life ended abruptly, without an opportunity for rethinking or for a course correction. And the way she had spent it serving others was profoundly more valuable than the way I might have wanted her to spend it. If she had an instant before her injury to consider how she had lived, she'd have had no reason for regret. I've heard people ask the question: "If you knew you had only one day left to live, how would you live it?" You probably wouldn't spend it doing the laundry. And that's how Carol Ann lived—as if each day were her last.

Tragedy changes your perspective, forever. It clarifies your vision so that you can better see the way things really are. In Carol Ann's case, she had always thought that compassion, generosity, and service to others were important. But after losing Cynthia Kate, it was as if the less-important things receded completely into the background, and the more important things, such as giving fully of her time and her emotion to those who needed them, filled her vision, enabling her to see clearly that this is what life was about.

When Jesus was asked which was the greatest commandment, he said,

"'Love the Lord your God with all your heart and with all your soul and with all your mind.' This is the first and greatest commandment. And the second is like it: 'Love your neighbor as yourself.' All the Law and the Prophets hang on these two commandments."

MATTHEW 22:37–40 NIV

All of that is pretty striking, but I find myself especially intrigued by that last line: "All the Law and the Prophets hang on these two commandments." Another way to say that might be, "This is the summation of the Law. These are the most important things you can do." And of the two things—just *two*—Jesus identifies as the most important things we can do, one is, "Love your neighbor as yourself." We tend to elevate other religious activities that sound more holy above the simple idea of serving others. But that's not what Jesus taught. He taught that how we treat other people is the pinnacle of Christian character. Carol Ann lived as if she believed that.

Years later, someone sent me an article called, "God Spares Not His Sons." The central idea of the article was that, in the Bible, there are many, many examples of men and women whom God did not spare the trauma of life—rather, he allowed them to experience the heartbreak and anguish and then, later, invited them to participate in his work in powerful ways as a result of it. Joseph in the Old Testament book of Genesis is a good example—he experienced one painful betrayal and setback after another for decades—but that allowed God to put him into a position of authority and influence from which he was able to help and even save the lives of thousands. Joseph's brothers, on the other hand, were spared that pain—they were the sons of a wealthy man and as a result lived comfortable, settled lives—but theirs were lives of mediocrity, and as a result, we remember little about them.

For myself, and certainly for my family, I tend like most people to pray that God would spare us from tragedy, from heartbreak. I wonder sometimes whether our prayers shouldn't sound more like, "Not my will, but yours, be done." We never know what God might be preparing us to do.

After Cynthia Kate, we tried again.

Two more miscarriages.

To say that those years of loss and disappointment and grief took a toll on us, and particularly on Carol Ann, is an understatement. Five years of tests, of pregnancies that didn't result in living babies that we could take home from the hospital and cuddle and smile over and show off and watch grow—what was wrong with us that we couldn't do the simple thing that couple after couple around the world and throughout history had been able to do? Many couples didn't *want* to have babies and did anyway.

Maybe we should stop trying, we thought. *Maybe we should stop with Jessica, be thankful for what we have, and forget having any more kids.*

We had tons of genetic testing done. One day we sat in the doctor's office as he said, "There's nothing wrong with either of you. I know you'd rather hear that I've found some correctable condition that has been creating these problems, but the simple truth is, our tests have come up with nothing. There's nothing wrong that is preventing you from having a baby. If you want more kids, you can have kids. There's no biological reason why this is happening. The choice is yours, of course, but you can always keep trying."

We decided to try one more time, and once again Carol Ann got pregnant. *Getting* pregnant had never been the problem.

When we went into the lab to get an ultrasound, we went in with the usual sense of dread. Something had gone wrong every time but one—what would it be this time? Would it show up in the ultrasound? We had spent hours praying before going to the lab, and I had said, "Carol Ann—if there's a problem, if this pregnancy ends, then let's just keep trying.

We've got one healthy child, so we know it can be done. Let's keep trying."

The technician moved the wand through the gel across Carol Ann's swollen belly and casually, as if discussing the weather, said, "Y'all know it's twins, right?"

We were stunned. Speechless.

She glanced up and saw the look on our faces. "Oh, my gosh—you didn't know, did you? I'm so sorry—I didn't realize this was your first ultrasound. But it's true—you have twins."

And what's more, the twins were, at that point at least, fine. What an incredible mixture of emotions we felt that day. Overjoyed that Carol Ann was carrying not one healthy baby but two! And yet knowing from repeated experiences that anything could go wrong, right up until the day of birth. We didn't know whether to laugh or cry, to cheer in exultation or scream in terror. Most likely at one time or another over the next few months, we did all four.

This was considered a high-risk pregnancy because of all her previous problems, so the doctor confined her to bed at about twenty weeks. We set up a bed in the kitchen; she could go downstairs once and upstairs once every day. She lay there in that kitchen bed every day, all day long. My sister Cynthia moved in with us and helped with Jessica, who was four.

Even though we felt some anxiety every day that something would go wrong, the pregnancy progressed normally and, about two weeks before she was due, the doctor decided to induce.

Even with the Pitocin, the delivery required hours and hours of waiting. Doctors and nurses were both checking her frequently, and eventually, after what seemed like an interminable wait, the nurse smiled and said, "It's time. I'll call the doctor. Let's have these boys!" She clicked on her little microphone and said, "It's time to deliver!"

The doors flew open almost as if the team had been waiting out in the hallway, and a roomful of medical professionals burst in. And not just the OB-GYN—because we were having twins, there were two of everything: two neonatologists, two anesthesiologists, and two pediatric everythings, ready to work on either baby once they were born. And they were all scrambling around, moving equipment, ripping open packages and sending the wrappings flying through the air like confetti. I'd already had one kid so I knew what it was like in a delivery room, but this was a whole different experience.

When the first of the twins emerged and seemed healthy, I couldn't believe how relieved I felt, as if the memories of Cynthia Kate's birth had been haunting me. The OB-GYN handed the first one off to the team of doctors there to look after him, took a few minutes for everyone to relax—close to eleven minutes, in fact, since that's how long there was between the two births—and then looked at Carol Ann and said, "Okay—are you ready for another one? Let's do it again."

When the frantic burst of activity was over, the result: two healthy boys, six-and-a-half pounds apiece—big for twins. It was unbelievable. We were overwhelmed, astonished. After all those years and so much anguish, there lay Jacob and Caleb.

And thus I found myself a couple of days later, in the middle of the night, standing over their bassinet at home with a silly grin on my face. It was really about the first chance I'd had to quietly enjoy them at my leisure, because the days at the hospital had been filled with both guests and medical people.

So much had gone wrong for so many years, there had been so much anguish through all of those pregnancies since Jessica's birth. Now here I stood, almost in disbelief, looking down at two healthy babies in a bassinet. It didn't erase the painful memories. It certainly didn't erase the memory of Cynthia Kate, nor would I want it to. But those memories were at least temporarily obscured by the brilliance of my gratitude that for these two all had gone so well, by the sense of blessing I felt that here they were breathing and with good color and with the doctor's confidence that they were healthy, by the magnitude of the fullness in my heart as I looked at my two sons after so much disappointment, so much heartache, so much struggle, so much fear.

Did we appreciate these babies more than someone might who hadn't gone through all the trouble we had? Yes—in my mind, there's no doubt. And the fact that there were two of them made it all the more glorious. As I stood there, my heart filled with gratitude—I was overwhelmed.

That moment illustrated to me the truth of something I would later remind the kids of after Carol Ann's death: That because of what we experienced as a family—in this case, the repeated loss of unborn children we longed for and loved— we would have a perspective and an understanding that other people who hadn't gone through what we had might not have.

Part of the joy I felt that night was for Carol Ann. How glad I was that, finally, she would be able to cuddle, kiss, and nurse these children of her own flesh, as she had Jessica five long years before. In unsuccessful pregnancy after unsuccessful pregnancy, much of my pain had come from watching her pain and knowing that there was nothing I could do about it, even though I so badly wanted to. For her to have been so disappointed for so long, to have gone through so much emotional turmoil ... now she had two babies to touch and love—once she woke up from her well-earned sleep.

I stood there grinning like a fool. And the boys have never given me a reason to stop grinning—the healthy babies turned into healthy children and healthy men.

Carol Ann and I decided that was enough—after so many heartbreaking failures, we had three healthy children. Let's not push our luck. We would stop at three.

But God had other plans, as he often does, and this time the plan was delightful. Five years later, we had a baby girl named Sarah Kate. We'd been happy with three—but God knew that Sarah Kate would bring new life to our family. The older children were thrilled to have a little sister to love on. And while Carol Ann and I may not have planned on Sarah Kate, soon we couldn't imagine life without her.

Life was rolling along far better than we had any right to expect. We had four thriving kids. My business was growing. As a family, we were prospering. I felt like the most blessed guy ever.

And then I came home one day and waved at Carol Ann as she crossed the creek on her horse with Sarah Kate on the saddle in front of her.

CHAPTER 7

A Birthday Rose

"I'm almost embarrassed to say this," I told my pastor, Don Finto, a week or so after the funeral, "but I'm surprised how well I'm doing."

It wasn't that I felt *good*. Far from it. But I was certainly doing better than I had expected. The first couple of days after her death were a blur—I was no doubt in shock. But after that, even though it was a struggle to stumble out of bed, I was doing it, and spending time with the kids and managing to eat something.

"I think," my pastor responded, "that at times like this the Lord cups his hands around us tightly. We're protected. And then as the days and weeks go by, he slowly opens his hands and allows us to start to experience the painful things we need to live through in order to become the people he wants us to be. But in those first few days, he extends a lot of grace."

He was absolutely right. A few days later, I hit a wall. Reality asserted itself. I would find myself waking up in the morning groggy and foggy, wondering, *What day is this? Was that all a nightmare?* And then, cruelly, the fog would clear and I would have to face all over again the reality that it had really happened, and that even so I had to get up and live with it. I had no choice—I had kids.

Little things hit you in the face. Like the first time you go downstairs to make coffee. For sixteen years, you've made coffee for two people. Now you realize like a kick in the face that you only need to make enough coffee for one.

After that, every day, you dread making coffee.

Going to bed at night. Exhausted as you are, you put off actually lying down to sleep as long as you can, because when you do, there will be no one beside you. So literally from the time you get up to the time you fall asleep, if you can, there will be unwelcome reminders of all you have lost.

You don't want to use up the shampoo, because that's the shampoo she used just last week. And once it's gone it will be gone forever. And you certainly don't want to move anything that was hers. There's her nightgown, right where she hurriedly took it off the last time and tossed it over the back of a chair. And you can't bring yourself to put it away, because never again will she wear it or hang it anywhere. You're surrounded on every side, hour after hour, by a terrible finality.

Two thousand people came to her funeral. I knew that her life had impacted a lot of others' lives, and I loved and admired her for it. But I didn't realize the extent of her influence until I saw them all packed in to honor her and to remember all that she had done and said. She didn't make that kind of impact by making sure the bills were paid, the house was clean, and the flowerbeds were beautiful. She did it by stepping out of her own comfort zone to address the needs of others, directly and intimately.

It was a simple service. I did her eulogy. My dad spoke about her. And my pastor. Her prayer group girls, a group of women she was very committed to and had walked with for years, sang. Michael W. Smith sang his well-known song "Friends," a song that had special meaning for Carol Ann and me. We had known Michael and his wife Debbie since all of us were in our early twenties. We all attended Belmont Church in Nashville, a church popular with Nashville musicians. We attended a Bible study with Michael and Debbie, who were newlyweds. Michael's career was just beginning—he was performing with Amy Grant but hadn't really experienced much success on his own. One night at Bible study, Michael said to the group, "We wrote a little song this afternoon—Debbie wrote the words and I wrote the music. We want to dedicate it to you all, because we love you. This is for you." And he sat down at the keyboard and played "Friends" for the first time it had ever been performed.

Of course, we loved it. And it became his most popular song. So his performing it at her funeral had special meaning. Later, Michael released an album called *Freedom* dedicated to Carol Ann. It includes an instrumental titled "Carol Ann."

One of my strongest memories of the funeral, though, actually came just before the service began, during the visitation period. I walked down the aisle of the church and stopped right behind my four kids sitting on the front row. The casket (closed) was right in front of them. They didn't know I was there.

I thought I had trusted God before, but until that moment I hadn't known the real meaning of the word *trust*. From that day forward, I had to trust God to work out a situation that had no possible way of working out.

I was aware, though, that I had one advantage. I'd had, up to that point, a lifetime of rehearsing for this by believing in what I could not see. Now I faced a challenge: How do I believe in a future that I can't even imagine without the wife who has been my partner all these years? I didn't know the answer to that question. I didn't even really understand that there could *be* an answer.

But I did know how to believe in something I couldn't see.

Carol Ann died two weeks before her forty-first birthday—which means that the rest of us had to somehow maneuver through that reminder of her while our wounds were still fresh and mostly unbound. Her parents came to help us all through it. It went better than I'd expected. But when it came time for them to leave, all four kids were away—they had gone to spend a night with various friends and relatives.

I stood on the driveway and watched Carol Ann's parents drive away. Then I turned and walked back to the house. No sooner had I put my hand on the back doorknob, though, than I froze and a wave of reality overtook me. I was about to enter alone the house we had created together, and she wasn't there, and she was never coming back.

So began the worst night of grief I ever experienced. I couldn't stop myself—I opened all of her drawers and went through her clothes, holding them to my face and smelling them. I opened and smelled her perfume. I wailed, I cried. The fact that there was no one there to hear me eliminated a constraint I'd hardly been aware of—I was completely alone, and my grief came shrieking out.

For the first time in my life, I understood how people some-times reach a state of hopelessness and despair that makes them want to kill themselves. Would I have even considered it, if only for a moment? No. But for the first time in my life, as I took stock of my tumultuous and miserable state of mind, I understood the feeling of those who make that choice. I had never experienced such hopelessness before, nor have I since.

I survived it. And, ironically, that night marked a begin-ning for us. I'd had two weeks of a high level of activity, so constantly surrounded by people, family, meals, letters, and emotions that I was never alone to face my own loss without distraction. Then a night of immersing myself in grief. And after that, subtly, things changed. My kids and I began, in at first just the slightest ways, hardly noticeably, to look—instead of back at the life we had lost—ahead to what came next. It was not the end of our grief—far from it, as I'll explain—but our grief became intentional. Our sorrow began to look forward. If our life during that period was a tapestry, it was a bleak and bitter one—but there was a thread of hope that wove subtly through it from that period on.

Many friends gave me, with the best of intentions, books to read. "This book helped me when my parents died—you should read it." Most of them I didn't read. But Dawn, a dear friend of Carol Ann's, gave me C.S. Lewis's book *A Grief Observed*. That book was profoundly helpful and had a huge impact on me. I opened it and found on the first page:

> No one ever told me that grief felt so like fear. I am not afraid, but the sensation is like being afraid. The same fluttering in the stomach, the same restlessness, the yawning. I keep on swallowing.
>
> (HARPERONE, 2015, P. 3)

I was stunned: *He knows exactly how I feel.* And that's rare. Those of us experiencing profound grief have the sensation that no one really knows what we're feeling. And we're mostly correct, because so much of what we feel in grief is intensely personalized. But just that first page was enough to tell me that C.S. Lewis really *did* know what I was experiencing. The whole book was that good—I underlined many places that are ridiculously powerful.

And many others who reached out to me did so compassionately and effectively.

A few months before Carol Ann's accident, a friend of ours, LeeAnn, called late one night and woke us up. Carol Ann answered, and I could tell by the tone of her voice and the look on her face that something terrible had happened. She hung up the phone and said, "Trisha just died. She had her fifth baby today and then died from some type of complication." Trisha's husband, Ron, was now left with five kids. We were shocked. I remember saying to Carol Ann, "What is he going to do? How in the world is he going to handle this with five kids?"

After we lost Carol Ann, I got hundreds of cards and notes and letters, and I kept them all and valued every one. But I remember the day I opened the one from Ron. I hung on every word of his letter. I was so grateful to have something in my hand from someone who knew what this felt like.

The two of us wrote back and forth. And those letters of his were so incredibly encouraging to me that it prompted me to start writing notes to other guys I heard about who had lost their wives.

Soon, I started seeing little signposts of hope nearly every day—things like a letter from Ron, or a positive sign about the kids, or some indication that things were starting to get easier, more "normal." I remember once hearing someone say that *hope* is something we believers offer the world that it can't easily find anywhere else. And hope is what began to put my life, and my kids' lives, back on track. And as the words of an old youth group song say, *Hope has a name: Jesus.*

One day I was standing on my back patio with a friend, and he said, "How long has it been since…?"

"Five weeks," I said, then paused to think, and added, "God, I wish it had been five months." I sat on a nearby chair and thought, *Will it ever be five years?* Because for the first time in my life, I wanted my life to hurry up and go by. I wanted my kids to grow up. I wanted it to be ten years from now. I didn't hate life, I didn't want to end mine—I just wanted to hurry up and get past the pain and on to whatever would come after. I wanted the future. Because I had enough hope to believe that whatever our future would hold, it would be good. But first we had to get past this. I just wanted the *now* to go away.

The thread of sweetness being woven into the bitterness of our days was powerful and palpable. I could taste it. Something terrible had happened to us—but in its aftermath, something remarkable was happening in us.

I began to seek out and study scriptures about struggle and difficulty. My understanding of God was rapidly changing. God was, I was coming to understand, less the orchestrator of my circumstances than he was the orchestrator of my heart. It wasn't that he was uninterested in my circumstances, but he was much more interested in my heart. And because of that, I believed that there was something bigger and more powerful going on in my life, and my kids' lives, than our circumstances.

It was that *something I could not see* that I had believed in standing before my wife's coffin at the funeral.

From the moment in Carol Ann's hospital room that I'd tried to reread that humbling passage from Job, I'd known that God was in this with me and that he was going to do something mighty and remarkable and beneficial. Something beyond my understanding. It's hard to be a Christian without believing in the supernatural, and in this case I not only believed in it—I desperately needed it.

And God would give me little reminders to help me keep up my faith and trust. Like Carol Ann's rose.

We had a little rosebush near the house that Carol Ann had planted about fifteen years before. It blooms in the spring, normally, not in August. But the first time Carol Ann's birthday came up just two weeks after her death, my sister came into the house and said, "There's a rosebud on Carol Ann's rosebush." We went out together and there it was, a single, salmon-colored rosebud—blooming in August, long after it should have stopped blooming. On Carol Ann's birthday. My sister took a picture of it and framed it for me. I've kept it ever since.

Hokey? Maybe. But I saw things like that as the ways God was reassuring me that something good was happening and that good things lay ahead for us. And since we lived surrounded by nature, those reassurances were usually natural things. Like a rosebud.

My pastor told me that God is nearest to us in birth and in death. He shows his hand on those occasions, perhaps just to remind us that he's there, and he does that in both natural and supernatural ways.

Frankly, I didn't require much in the way of supernatural signs of God's continuing care. I was reassured enough by the outpouring of support from my family, my friends, my parents. One afternoon that first fall after we lost Carol Ann, I came home and my dad was spreading grass seed on the steep bank behind my house. I always seeded my yard in the fall, by hand, and fertilized it then as well. My dad knew that because he usually went with me to the co-op, and we would buy seed together. When I saw him working on that back bank, I knew exactly what he was up to—he and my mom wanted to do something to help, but often didn't know exactly what. So— just do something. Seed the back bank. It would save me some work, and it would be a reminder of how much they cared and that I was on their mind.

That first school year after, my mother would get up every morning at 6:00, drive the short distance to my house, fix breakfast, and help me get the kids ready for school. And stand there in the driveway as we drove away, just as Carol Ann used to. And she did that every schoolday morning for the next *five years.* Again, so bittersweet—sweet that my mother was there to help, but bitter that it wasn't Carol Ann.

School started that first fall far too soon for us—only about three weeks after Carol Ann died. I drove to the school parking lot the day before school just to get the pain and grief out of the way. I couldn't stand the thought of driving in there with my kids on the first day and breaking down from grief. The parking lot was nearly empty that day, fortunately—just a couple of teachers there getting ready for the next day. I sat in the truck in a far corner of the lot and wept, dreading the next morning when I would drive my kids to school.

Shortly after, my sister Abby and her husband John, who have no children and had for several years been living on his own family's farm, moved back to my family's farm. She took over the role of caretaker of my kids in the afternoons. She would be at my house when the kids got home from school. Then she would fix dinner and set the table, and when I came home she would have already left, so that the kids and I would have the evening to ourselves. The role Abby played in my kids' lives is difficult to describe—much more than a caretaker.

Abby didn't always have to *cook* our dinners—women from church and from school fixed meals for my family. They had it all scheduled and organized, as women do during times of need. And they did it for a long, long time—two years, in fact—until we finally explained that, as much as we appreciated it, we didn't need that any more.

In the weeks after Carol Ann's funeral, I chose one person for each of my kids and asked them, "Would you be my child's go-to person? They'll need someone besides me that they'll know is happy to spend time with them and who will take their feelings and questions seriously." And I had no problem signing people up for that service.

Sarah Kate, the youngest, had of course up until Carol Ann's death been home with her mom all the time. I didn't want to put her in daycare. We found a little preschool program that provided a few hours of interaction a day, and after that she stayed with my mom. One woman, a good friend, offered to come stay at my house every Friday with Sarah Kate. In fact, she and her husband said, "We'll come over and keep your kids every Friday night. If you don't mind, we'll just stay overnight in the guest room. It's something we can do for the kids—and also for you. You can go out and you won't have to watch the clock."

And on those "free" Friday nights, I would usually go to the gym and then out to dinner and a movie with Lynn, my best friend, a brother I'd known for many, many years. Our relationship ran deep, and he was remarkably valuable to me through that season, and still is today.

Kim and Alan, who lived a few miles away, played a signifi-cant role for years: keeping my kids but, much more than that, loving them and making them part of their family.

I could relate story after story of the ways in which others contributed to our well-being. And the fact that my extended family mostly lived close by was a profound gift. My kids were not at all alone. They had cousins and aunts and uncles and grandparents who all lived close. Even now, my kids still have that network of family around them.

I'm aware how unusual it is, in the twenty-first century, that our family tends to stay connected and that we're all com-mitted to the value in that extended family connection—and not only that, but we're still geographically close. I mean *really* close. There's something very stabilizing and secure in hav-ing your grandparents' house, and your aunts and uncles, and your cousins, all just down the road. How rare is it, in our mobile society, that not only am I still living on the same piece of property, the same farm, where I grew up and have lived nearly all of my life, but that the other houses on the farm (nine of them!) are still occupied by my extended family and my kids. When so much is changing in your life, when there's so much chaos and turmoil, it's a comfort for there to be that certainty.

That's part of what faith offers, as well. A believer walk-ing through crisis has an anchor that can't be moved. When you're desperate for something solid and unchangeable to cling to, something firm, something secure, something that you can depend on no matter what—that anchor holds.

As the months went by, I came first to accept and then to embrace the idea that this might be both the worst and the best time of my life, and certainly the most important and consequential time. Something big was happening to me and to my kids. It was a lesson that cost us so much in pain and loss that there's no way I wanted to miss whatever growth or character development came with it.

I often told them during those months, "The four of you are experiencing something that most kids will never know—and because of that, as adults you will know things that most adults will never know and understand things that most adults will never understand. If you just stay close to God and allow him to be part of that process, then the things you are experiencing now, as painful as they are, will guide you in a positive direction. You will be uniquely gifted adults—not *despite* this terrible experience that you're going through, but *because* of it." I must have told them that a hundred times. And I believe every word of it. About my kids, and about myself.

I even started to look at scripture differently. Jesus talked about the *abundant life*. I used to think of abundant life as being happy, joyful, certain, peaceful. But in the months after losing Carol Ann, as I would read my Bible I began to see true abundance as being joyful in the midst of grief. Having peace in the midst of chaos. Certainty in the midst of uncertainty. I began to think of the abundant life as rising above your circumstances, as walking in fullness even when life is falling apart around you. Impossible? In the months so soon after Carol Ann's accident, I sometimes wondered. It didn't feel possible to me, but I came more and more to be sure that this is what Jesus came to give us. "'In this world you will have trouble,'" Jesus told his disciples. "'But take heart! I have overcome the world.'" (John 16:33, NIV). Clearly, if he was telling his disciples that they would have trouble here on earth, then he wasn't planning to clear the road of any difficulties—he expected them to face them and learn and grow from them.

In fact, as James reminds us:

Consider it pure joy, my brothers and sisters, whenever you face trials of many kinds, because you know that the testing of your faith produces perseverance. Let perseverance finish its work so that you may be mature and complete, not lacking anything.

James 1:2–4

We should not only accept troubles in life—we should consider it a joy to face them, knowing that we will grow through them.

I'm going to have trouble in life. I know that—I dread it, but I know it's coming anyway. I can ask God to spare me from it when he will, but that's a prayer he has already told me he's not always going to answer *yes*. So when those troubles come, I am going to wring from them every life lesson, every exercise of my character that results in me being a better man. The cost is high and I want to reap the benefit.

Top: My family in about 1961 when I was a toddler in my father's arms.

Bottom: My parents Wallace and Ann Lee.

Top left: My grandparents Leon and Joyce Lee with my sister Cynthia.
Top Right: My grandfather Leon and I.
Bottom left and right: Early photos of Lee Company.

Top: A Bartholomew family reunion at the home of my grandparents on my mother's side, Byron and Cleo Bartholomew, at their home on Adams Avenue in downtown Memphis. (I'm in the white shirt kneeling in the first row, third in from the right.)

Bottom: My family with Carol Ann on our front porch at the farm, about 1998.

Top: I'm with Steven and Abby showing off our prize calves.
Bottom left: Our close neighbors Mr. and Mrs. Cliff Linton.
Bottom right: My brother Steven with Mr. Linton and his 1951 Chevy pickup.

Showing my 4-H calf at the Tennessee State Fairgrounds.

Sarah Kate and I showing her state champion Hereford heifer in 2008.

Sarah Kate with a plaque and ribbon in 2012.

Top: I'm proud of a new Lee Company truck in 1997.
Bottom left: My dad took my brother Steven and me on a hunting trip to the Yukon when I was eighteen.
Bottom right: Here I am with my siblings—Carol, Cynthia, Steven, and Abby.

Carol Ann and I with the kids in front of our rented RV
on our Yellowstone trip in July 2000.

One of my favorite photos of our family on the July 2000 trip with the Tetons looming in the background.

The beginning of my life as a single dad. At Seaside in 2001 and in the snow at our farm in 2002.

Climbing the Grand Teton with Jessica for her sixteenth birthday in 2002.

Top: Caleb's third-grade class with with Miss DiNenna in 1999-2000. (Caleb is on the middle row second from the left.)
Bottom left and right: Maria with Jessica and Sarah Kate in the early years.

Carol Ann's and Cynthia Kate's markers in the family cemetery.

Top: The kids and I in Nairobi, Kenya, in 2008.
Bottom: Our flight to Gulu, Uganda.

Maria and I in 2014.

Maria's and my wedding at our farm on October 18, 2008.
op: The Lee extended family.   Bottom: The DiNenna extended family.

Maria and I with our five grandkids. The youngest three were born within a month of each other at the end of 2017.

CHAPTER 8

A LIFE PRESERVED

First everythings are hard after the loss of a loved one, because it's the first time you've done it without them. There's an empty chair at the kitchen table.

We lost Carol Ann in July, and my grief wobbled downhill from then until Thanksgiving, when it hit bottom. I'm not a drinking man but I've frequently told people that I drank my way through that first Thanksgiving, and that isn't far off the truth. Our tradition during the years of our marriage was to celebrate Thanksgiving with my family on Wednesday night, drive to Carol Ann's parents' house in Birmingham that night and arrive late, then celebrate Thanksgiving day with Carol Ann's family at their big family gathering at their lake house. All of Carol Ann's relatives would be there, including her sisters and cousins. After Thanksgiving dinner we would build a bonfire near the lake, and there we'd spend the afternoon. That evening we would spend at Grandmother's house and stay the night there. So Thanksgiving was a Person family event.

And that's one reason I dreaded it that first year after.

But I was determined to do it. I wanted to change the kids' holiday traditions as little as possible, trying to minimize the number of things they were losing. Even if it killed me, we would celebrate Thanksgiving in the place and in the manner we always did. It almost felt to me as if Thanksgiving was a roadblock we had to jump over. So we did.

I tend to approach life that way. When you face something difficult, just go headlong into it. I thought it was best to face grief head on. If everyone was thinking it, then you might as well say it. Just get it out of the way.

For instance, the following summer we spent a vacation week at the same house we'd rented with Carol Ann the year before, her last year with us, painful memories or not. Later that summer, we rented an RV and went to Yellowstone, just as we'd done mere weeks before her accident. Painful? Yes, incredibly painful for me and for all of us I'm sure. But it was how I approached grief—dive into it and get it over with.

That first Christmas after her death, too, I dreaded, but on Christmas Eve I was pleasantly surprised. It wasn't that bad. If my grief had bottomed out at Thanksgiving, maybe now I was on the way up. Maybe this was doable.

There's a scripture in Isaiah (1:18) that says, "'Though your sins are like scarlet, they shall be as white as snow.'" Every time it snowed, I would tell my kids that the snow covers all of the darkness and dirtiness and brown left from the previous year. Everything gets covered over and made beautifully white. And that's a picture of what God does for us. And on

New Year's Day it snowed—a heavy snow, by Tennessee standards. It was an extremely hopeful day for me. My friend Lynn, the one I worked out with on Friday nights, and I took a long walk together across the farm in the snow. We prayed for new beginnings. That afternoon, I went sledding with the kids. The old year was now gone, thank God. Surely the next one would be better.

But of course, as the first anniversary of her death approached—July 22nd of 2001—I was uneasy. More than uneasy—I dreaded it. As those little indicators in nature began to appear—certain flowers in bloom, the trees taking on a certain shade of green, the cicadas buzzing—my emotions were on edge. It's not that I had a premonition that something bad was going to happen, I just didn't want those reminders to cause us all to relive more intensely in our minds and hearts what had happened a year before, and what was daily in our minds anyway.

We made it through the one-year anniversary. But sometime that fall, something started happening with Jessica, my oldest daughter. And I wasn't sure what it was.

Like all of us, she'd been doing much better. She'd been the very happy, hopeful, successful, beautiful young girl she'd been before her mom's death, a girl for whom life was good. Because she was the oldest, the one best able to process things and discuss them as an adult would, I'm sure I put more on her than I should have. I treated her as if she were the other adult in the house. But she *wasn't* an adult. She was fourteen years old when her mother died.

By fall of 2001, she had turned fifteen and was moving toward sixteen. In the helpless, clueless way of most parents of adolescents, I felt as if I saw more danger signs every week, but had no idea how to address them. And the relationship between the two of us that had been so strong and open for so long was rapidly shutting down.

The story I tell in this chapter may revolve around an important event in my daughter Jessica's life, but it's not my place to tell Jessica's story. Only she knows and can tell that, and I'm sure I would do an inadequate job if I tried. Instead, what you'll read in this chapter is the story of how that event in Jessica's life affected me, because that's the only part of the story I'm qualified to tell. My daughter's story is powerful and redemptive and far too complex and detailed to be told in one chapter. She is on her own journey—as a strong, creative, and successful person, as a nurse, as a wife, as a mother of three and a remarkably gifted woman. Someday I hope that she will tell that story herself, and when she does I hope that she will give her own account of the circumstances, the emotions, and the complexities that led to the events of this chapter. I love her deeply and am grateful for who she has become, for the relationship we have, and for her story, which is still being written and yet to be told.

On February 19, 2002, I was working at my desk when my assistant, Debbie, her voice filled with distress, called from her desk just outside my office: "Bill, your mom is on the phone— you have to answer this now!" All of my calls at work ring on Debbie's line.

I hurried out to Debbie's desk and took the phone. Mom was hysterical. "You have to come home!" she cried. "Now!"

"What is it?"

"It's Jessica. She's hurt herself. Come home now!"

"What do you mean? Hurt herself how?"

A brief pause, then: "She just hurt herself."

You can tell when someone is trying hard to not say the words that they know will devastate you. It was much like when I had called Charlie, Carol Ann's father, on the night of Carol Ann's horseback riding accident. He had answered the phone with effervescent goodwill—"Hello, Bill!"—and I thought, *I don't want to do this. I don't want to say these words because his life will never be the same after I say them.* Speaking the words that will forever change someone's life, and not for the better, is a terrible thing. And I knew that that's exactly what Mom was fighting. But I had to know. "Mom, tell me. How did she hurt herself?"

"She shot herself!" She was crying so hard I could barely make out her words. "Come home! Please! Quickly!"

"Shot herself? Where—in the foot?"

My mom said, "No—she shot herself in the head. We called the ambulance."

I hung up the phone. Debbie said, "What happened? What happened?" I didn't answer—just walked back into my office and shut the door. I couldn't believe it. I just couldn't believe this was happening. I was in a suit and tie, but I lay down on the floor. I thought, *I'm done. I can't get up.* I lay there a few minutes in shock and disbelief and didn't know what to do.

Debbie kept knocking on the door, knocking on the door, and that's what finally got me up. I opened the door; Debbie and a couple of other people were standing there, shocked and concerned. I walked past them down the hall toward the parking lot. Someone said, "I'll go with you."

"Nobody's going with me," I said.

I walked out to the parking lot, got into my car, and started driving home. I called my mom on my cell: "Where is she going?"

She said, "She's going to Vanderbilt. The helicopter is on its way."

"I'll just meet you at Vanderbilt."

I turned around and headed back out to I-65 North toward Vanderbilt University Medical Center. I couldn't believe it: Here I was chasing another Life Flight helicopter to Vanderbilt. Just when I had gotten to where I could stand up again, I get hit in the back of the head with a 2 x 4. I had the most overwhelming, panicked sense that my life was spiraling out of control.

Driving up I-65, I was completely overwhelmed by the emotions whirling through my head. But one thought, one idea, pierced the confusion, the only clear thought I could find: I should worship.

I started singing. Worship songs. I don't remember which ones, but I sang them. In the car, by myself, driving to Vanderbilt. Spontaneously. It's all I could think to do. It was the only thing that made any sense whatsoever at that moment.

When I was on my way to Vanderbilt after Carol Ann's accident, I stopped and picked up some chewing tobacco. I did it because when nothing makes sense, you do whatever comes to your head. I think my singing worship songs as I drove to Vanderbilt for Jessica was much the same. You have to do something. And nothing else made sense.

I drove up 21st Avenue, and as I approached the hospital, I saw the helicopter sweep in, hover, and then land on the roof. It was surreal. And shocking. There was the Life Flight helicopter landing on the roof of the hospital, once again—only this time it's carrying my daughter and I don't know even know if she's dead or alive.

Once again I walked into the building. Once again I stepped onto the elevator and punched the button to the 11th floor. But this time when I met the doctor, the message was different: "She's going to live," he said. "We don't know the extent of the injuries. Brain injuries are complex—we don't yet know whether any damage might be permanent. But she's going to make it."

Parents understand that nothing in life hits you harder than the things that harm your children, even when they do it to themselves. My emotions were on overload. I didn't know what to do and didn't know what would come next, but I knew we had just launched ourselves onto a whole new journey, and it was one I had no clue how to navigate.

But there was still one more task I had to find my way through—I had to go home that night and tell Jessica's siblings about the events of that afternoon. To say that was hard for us all would be an understatement. Once again, we found ourselves huddled together on the floor—this time in Jacob and Caleb's bedroom—and crying ourselves to sleep.

She spent a week in the hospital. She had some brain swelling and other physical issues resulting from the injury, but the prognosis was good. At least Jessica's was—I'm not sure about mine.

Early one morning while she was still in the hospital, I came downstairs and sat in my living room and started to pray. I was terrified, I was confused, as I'd been every day and every night since I got Mom's panicked phone call. I had just spent over a year desperately trying to single-handedly manage life so that everybody would be okay. I was the widower who could take care of every child's problem, make sure all of them were getting what they needed—getting their schoolwork done, getting enough nurturing, getting enough of my time. And then it all blew up. I couldn't do any more than I was, and yet obviously it wasn't working.

In some ways, I felt as if we'd gone back to go and were starting all over, as if we'd accomplished nothing in the more than a year since losing Carol Ann. *What am I supposed to do, Lord?* I prayed.

Sometimes when you pray, it's as if God speaks back. Everybody processes that differently. On this particular morning as I poured out my fears and doubts, it was as if God were saying to me, "She's mine."

I remember sitting up straighter, because the sense of getting a response was so strong—and also because the response itself threw me. My daughter had just tried to kill herself a few days before—and now God is telling me that she's his? What is he saying? Is he going to let her succeed?

I envisioned God sitting in the chair opposite me, and I pointed at the chair and said, "Then if she dies, it's your fault."

"And if she lives it's because I save her, not you," I sensed his reply.

And surprisingly, rather than feeling guilt, I felt a burden lifting. I'd been nearly a year and a half accepting personal responsibility for making sure that all my kids were going to be okay—and clearly I'd failed. But I'd just been reminded that someone a whole lot wiser and more powerful than me was also shouldering responsibility for my kids. *If my kids are going to be okay,* I prayed, *it's because you are going to make them okay. I'll do my best. I'll keep working hard. But from this day on, I'm going to trust you with my kids and their future.*

You can't protect a child from herself 24/7 for the rest of her life if she's determined to do herself harm. I had been feeling the incredible pressure of trying to do that. Knowing that the best I could do was enough lifted a huge burden from me.

For me, as for many parents, this marked the first time I'd had to work to understand depression and the daily struggle of those subject to it. That might have been much harder for me had I not experienced, just a year and a half before in the immediate wake of Carol Ann's death, a night of utter despair and hopelessness—a night when I understood for the first time what leads people to take their own lives.

Jessica's recovery, as with all people subject to depression, didn't happen overnight. But I can point to certain milestones in it, and one very important one that happened as soon as she came home from the hospital really marks, at least in my mind, the point at which her recovery began. As soon as we pulled up to the house, I said, "There's something I'd like for us to do."

And I led her back to the place in the house where her suicide attempt had taken place. She was reluctant, but I said, "Trust me on this, please." I asked her to sit on a chair in the middle of the room. Then I brought in a tub of water. I removed her shoes and socks and, kneeling on the floor, with tears in her eyes and mine, I washed her feet. As I did, I said, "Jessica, I'm doing this because I want you to know that your father will do whatever it takes—*whatever* it takes—to make sure that we get through this. I can't make you okay. That's God's responsibility, not mine. But I will serve you however you need me to to make that happen."

Over the next days and weeks, I could feel her healing begin in earnest. And I could sense that this tragic experience in Jessica's life had begun the process of creating a powerful woman with deep understanding. She told me, "When things were going from bad to worse for me, I never stopped talking to God—I just stopped listening to him. For the rest of my life I want to listen."

Life was on its way to being good again.

CHAPTER 9

THE FAMILY BUSINESS

My grandfather, Leon Lee, had eleven brothers and sisters and a third-grade education. He grew up in Dickson County, Tennessee, a descendant of a long line of Lees who initially settled in Tennessee in 1796. He taught himself to work on compressors and refrigeration equipment and as a young man moved to Nashville to work as a mechanic. In 1944, when he was in his mid-thirties, he started a company called Lee Refrigeration Service Company, working out of a Chevy sedan with the backseat taken out—that was his "truck." He worked on equipment such as compressors, milk coolers, and beer coolers.

His two sons, my dad Wallace and my uncle Ted, both went to Vanderbilt and got degrees in mechanical engineering, then both served in the military. My dad worked for a while at DuPont, and in the 1960s, both sons came back to work in their dad's business. When Grandpa died of a heart attack, my dad, who was seven years older than his brother, took over the business. Even then it was a small business with only a dozen or so employees, but my dad and uncle started growing it. First, he expanded into designing, installing, and maintaining

144

HVAC (heating, ventilation, and air conditioning) systems. In the 1970s, they bought a plumbing company and then an electrical company.

While I was in college, I worked at the company during the summers. I started as a mechanic's helper working on a truck with an HVAC service technician. I also worked as an apprentice to a draftsman and got a master plumber's license. I graduated from Auburn with a mechanical engineering degree and came to work at Lee Company full time in 1981, right out of college. I held, in succession, several positions in the company and grew to love this business—but mostly I grew to love the employees I worked with. The people who make up our company are mostly skilled tradesmen—men and women who are remarkably gifted at what they do. I have developed a deep appreciation for the people who make this country work, and at Lee Company, who serve our customers in the most remarkable ways.

I became the president of the company in 1992. We had about 150 employees then and did about $20 million in business. I bought my dad and uncle out in 1999. This year we have about 1250 employees and we'll do about $240 million in revenue.

I have been blessed to be part of a family business with such a rich legacy. Not only was I able to work alongside my father and my uncle, but I also have had the privilege of taking a business and growing it to where it is today. Our mission statement says, "Our job is to create an environment where people can thrive." That has become a lifelong mission of mine. That's why I was so proud when Lee Company was chosen just last year as the best company to work for in Nashville. We have exceptional employees, and it has been my privilege to work beside them for thirty-five years to create a company we are all deeply proud of. But as in life, the journey of this company, from its founding till today, has not always been smooth.

In the spring of 2003, I decided to run a marathon. I took off every Friday to train. Frankly, I needed the break—I was feeling overwhelmed. Given everything my family had been through in the three years previous, and given that I had the responsibility to shepherd four kids through those tough times, I was exhausted.

It was, I thought, a good time to take off—the company seemed to be booming. I had put in place leadership I trusted to run the company, and I had left the reins completely in their hands since I had stepped away from day-to-day operation when Carol Ann passed. So for a few months I worked four days a week and trained one day, and ran a marathon in April.

It was certainly the most hope-filled, exciting, positive spring I'd had in three or four years.

But when, after the marathon, I returned to the company, the partner who'd been running the company left, and I found myself having to take back day-to-day operations. By that time, we had opened an office in Birmingham and one in Orlando, and we were employing about eight hundred people.

So at the dinner table that night, I said, "Hey, guys—Dad has had a lot of time off from work the last few years. And that's all been great. And now that we're all in a good place and things are going in the right direction, I'm going back to work."

So in July of 2003, after having been less than fully engaged with the running of Lee Company for a few years, I jumped in with both feet. I remember the day I walked back into the office, no longer just as owner and CEO but now once again as the guy who ran things. It was time to reengage, and I loved it. I love everything about this company. I love what we do, and I love the people who do it. I had never really wanted to disengage after Carol Ann's death—I just didn't feel I could function in the midst of all that emotional turmoil.

But by September, I'd seen enough to know that the company was in deep financial trouble—and had been for some time. I kept looking at the numbers, and they weren't making sense. On paper it appeared that we were profitable, but according to the bank we had a serious cash flow problem.

We had monthly financial accountability meetings at which we reviewed the figures on each major job. We had three major projects going—one in South Carolina, one in Alabama, and another in Texas. None of the three was performing well, and one was really going down the tube. In preparation for one monthly meeting, I asked my managers for a full report, diving deep—I wanted to really know what was happening.

When I walked into the meeting that day, there were ten managers there and the numbers for one of the three contracts were up on the board. As my managers began to explain the numbers, there was a lot of hemming and hawing, as if they were telling me what they thought I wanted to hear instead of what was really going on. I pointed to the numbers on the board and said, "You need to be completely honest with me. I want to know exactly where you think this job is going to end up. Don't kid me. Don't kid yourself. I want to know the truth."

The project manager said, "Well, here's what I *think* is going to happen." He put a number up on the board. I'd known that we were going to take a loss on the project, but the manager's projection showed a loss a couple million dollars deeper than any previous projections had shown. I knew what it meant for the company—and for me. We had already lost a lot of money that quarter. We had multiple jobs going south. We were cash-poor, and we had maxed out our credit at the banks. If we took another two-million-dollar hit, the company might not survive it.

And yet there it was, written on the board.

I backed my chair away from the table and looked down at the floor in disbelief.

This was not just some company. This was my grandfather's company, the one he had started working out of the back of his car. Lee Company. It bore my name.

When someone else's company goes bankrupt, you can shrug it off and find another job somewhere else—but when the company founded by your family and named after your family goes bankrupt, it's personal. If Lee Company went belly up, eight hundred families—eight hundred families that depended on Bill Lee to protect their livelihood—would lose their source of revenue. And it would be my fault. I would have to face the employees and explain that they were going to lose their jobs. I would have to explain to the members of my own extended family that Lee Company, the company that Grandpa and Dad and Uncle Ted had grown and kept healthy for decades, was now going to come crashing down on Bill Lee's watch.

And it would all happen this fall.

Nobody in the room said a word. I stared at the floor for about three minutes, trying numbly to comprehend that what I had just seen on the board would change forever my life and probably everybody else's in the room.

I stood up and I walked out. I walked out the front door to the parking lot, got into my car, and drove to a nearby park at the top of a hill, to a quiet place I sometimes went to pray or contemplate or think, or even just to eat lunch when I needed some solitude. I took out a big chew of tobacco—I was still dipping in 2003—and I said, "Okay, God, we've had several tough chapters, several struggles, in the Lee family story over the past few years. I guess this is the next one."

Our line of credit was exhausted—we had borrowed all the money we could borrow. We were already living hand-to-mouth on receivables and payables. Saving the company would take more than a few phone calls, more than a plan—it would take a campaign.

I spent days, frenzied days, preparing for that campaign. I talked with my dad about it, and he helped me navigate through it. As a businessman most of his adult life, he'd certainly been through financial struggles of his own. Then I called my five largest suppliers and asked each to come into my office one at a time. I had stayed up night after night developing a cash-flow plan, and I knew that it *could* work—but not without cooperation from everybody, not just within the company but also our banks and suppliers. And everything would have to go right, because the company was on the verge of collapse.

Meeting with each supplier individually, I put all of my charts and graphs up on the screen and showed them how my plan could work. Then I asked each of my five major suppliers to extend their credit for our company to 180 days. Normally, we would pay them in thirty days, or maybe sixty or even ninety if things were really slow. I said, "I can't pay you any more right now. But I *can* pay you in 180 days. Suspend your receivables and allow me to not pay you for the next six months. But continue to do business with us. I *will* start paying you."

If they cut me off, I would go broke and they wouldn't get paid at all. These were all people I'd done business with for a long time and had long-term relationships with—but even so, there was no guarantee that they would cooperate.

Never before had I experienced business stress like that. Until we had everyone's agreement—and even after, as with great difficulty we made the plan work—I had to keep reminding myself: *Nobody is dying here. And I know what it's like when someone dies. So keep it in perspective.*

Life for me has been a long exercise in keeping things in perspective.

Some days were worse than others. One day when things were at their most troubling, I thought I was having a heart attack. I called my buddy who's a cardiologist and said, "Dick, I think I'm having a heart attack. Like right now."

"No, you're not," he said. "Tell me what's going on."

"I've got some real deep problems in the business, and I just today got some really bad news from my bonding company. I've really been under a lot of stress. I don't sleep at night. I've got chest pains—I think I'm having a heart attack."

He said again, "No, you're not." He asked me a list of questions about symptoms and then he said, "I want you to go home—give yourself permission to lie down and rest for an hour or two. Then call me tonight and tell me if you feel worse."

When I called him that evening, I said, "Well, I don't feel any worse."

He said, "You're not having a heart attack. But come into the office tomorrow and we'll check it out."

His diagnosis the next day: "You've got acid reflux."

I wonder how many times in a year cardiologists make that same diagnosis. They might put the gastroenterologists out of business.

How did things go so badly wrong? Remember: Our success as a company is based as much on cash flow as it is on yearly revenues. At the time things went south, we had revenue of about $100 million a year. And we had about $30 million tied up in those three big jobs. We had grown very rapidly in the previous three or four years. And rapid growth requires capital. We were already leveraged pretty heavily because we were self-funding all of that growth. And that works fine—as long as you're making a profit. But when we had not only one job but three major jobs all get into trouble at the same time, and when we already, as a result of so much rapid growth, had too many new employees, too many new managers, too many new offices....

We lost three million dollars in three months. For a company our size operating on a 2 or 3 percent operating margin, that was a major blow. It wasn't a matter of going bankrupt as much as it was a cash crisis. We didn't have the cash to survive.

Fortunately we still had business—we were doing jobs and getting paid for them. There was enough revenue coming in that, with careful, diligent management, we could make my plan work. But week to week, month to month, it was incredibly challenging and stressful. There were frequent phone calls:

"You haven't paid my bill yet. When am I going to get paid? I have employees of my own to pay, you know."

"I've heard some things about your company. Are you going bankrupt?"

"Sorry—based on what I've been hearing about Lee Company, I can't award you this contract. I can't be confident you'll be in business long enough to complete the work. You might leave me high and dry with a half-completed job."

It builds on itself. Once word gets out that you're having trouble—and I couldn't deny it—the dominoes start to fall. Our bank thought the odds were good that we were going to fail, so they put us in what they call "special assets." Which is a terrible thing to happen to a business. Our bonding company agreed, so they wouldn't write us any more bonds. And for a construction company, if you can't get bonding, then you generally can't get contracts for work. So I had to negotiate with other companies to get bonding.

I had to do a lot of selling in those months, a lot of explaining—not to mention a lot of hoping and praying. I knew that with the new work we had coming in, if we could keep those new projects profitable and if everyone would show us some grace for six months, we would make it.

My kids picked up on my stress.

One night at dinner, Caleb said, "Hey, Dad—are we going bankrupt?"

I thought about how to answer. "Well, I don't know," I said finally. "We might be. So let's talk about it."

I definitely had their attention.

"If we did go bankrupt, here's what would probably happen. We would probably have to move. But not off the farm. We would probably have to sell this house. You know that mobile home the Jensens lived in while they were having their house built?" The Jensens, who were then and still are dear friends, had kids about the ages of my kids, so my kids had often been over to their place to play.

Sarah Kate said, "I loved that house, that was awesome. But it's not there anymore."

"That one's gone. But we would probably move into one something like it. Here on the farm." I paused for a minute for them to digest that idea. "We'd probably stop going to CPA." That was Christ Presbyterian Academy, the private school my kids went to. "We wouldn't go to Seaside anymore." That's where we went on vacation in Florida. A very nice place but expensive, and I was sure that if I lost the company, I wouldn't be able to afford it.

I said, "We probably wouldn't go to Disney World anytime soon. And we wouldn't have a lot of money to spend. We wouldn't buy as much stuff. We could keep what we have, like our four-wheelers, and we could still live on the farm. I might change jobs and go work somewhere else. But that's about it. We'd still be together. We'd go to church on Sundays and then over to Grandma's for lunch. It would be a lot like it is now except that we wouldn't have as much money."

They all looked thoughtful, and finally they nodded. "Okay."

That little talk wasn't just for their benefit. It helped me too. For the next year as we eased the company out of trouble, I often said to myself, *If we go bankrupt, we'll all still sit around the table together and eat dinner.* The kids weren't the only ones who needed reassurance. Life goes on and can still be a good life even when things don't work out the way you want them to.

All of our suppliers and creditors signed on to the deal I'd proposed.

Now we had to be diligent in keeping up our end. Every Thursday afternoon, I would walk into my CFO's office and ask her if she'd figured out a way to make tomorrow's payroll work.

One day when things looked dire, I walked into our Franklin main office and I sat down with one of my top managers to decide which employees we were going to keep and who we would have to let go. It was so difficult. "Can we keep Mary, or should it be Joe? She's been here twenty years and he's been here eighteen. He's got a kid. She's a single mom."

You want to keep everyone. These aren't just names on a page. These are people you hired because you believed in their ability, people who have now become friends, in some cases for many years. People who believed in and trusted in your ability to keep the company going, whose livelihood, whose ability to put food on the table and clothe their kids and keep a roof over their heads, depended on it. People who have worked hard for you and done a good job. People whose families you know. But it's either let many of them go or lose the company so that everyone has to go.

Then you have to call Mary and Joe and all the rest of them into the office and say, "Today's your last day." And it's dreadful.

Then I had to drive to the Birmingham office, and I spent the three hours of the drive trying to choose the words I would use to once again tell people something that would change their lives. I had to stand up in front of every Birmingham employee of our company that day and say, "I'm sorry, but we're going to close this office. All of you are going to lose your jobs."

And I went to Orlando and said the same thing.

We laid off four hundred workers in fourteen months. Four hundred. That's half of our employees—let go. And in order to stay financially healthy, to operate at a level we could maintain with a healthy cash flow, we actually cut our company revenue from about $100 million to $67 million the next year. We sold a building. We sold everything we didn't need.

And when we were as lean as we could get, and stable, then we punched the reset button.

By the fall of 2004, about a year after the crisis began, we knew we had made it. We had survived. (I say *we* because, through this process, I'd found a right-hand man—a manager who had been in our company for years and who stepped up and proved himself to be a strong leader, working by my side and helping me to guide the company through the hardest of times. Richard today serves as the CEO of the company I chair, and more importantly he has become a lifelong friend.)

We were a much smaller, leaner company. And a financially healthy one again.

I confess: There were times in the process when I looked back over my family's life in the previous few years and thought,

Wow. Really? Now this? After everything else we've faced, everything we've lost—how much is too much? But we survived it.

The company started making money again, started being profitable again. We started growing the company again—but more slowly and more intentionally this time. Like the employees who'd managed to keep their jobs throughout the struggle, I was grateful that I'd survived the storm. We started hiring people back, starting with some of those we'd let go, if they were still available.

Slowly, I began to feel hopeful again. I was very, very tired—but it was the beginning of a good season for me. There's nothing like a clear day after days of storm. Nothing like that feeling you get that first warm day in February. That's what it felt like. I had never appreciated a clear day so much.

You don't know wholeness until you've experienced brokenness. You don't laugh quite as hard—or enjoy it more—unless you have cried really deeply.

The best year the company ever had was 2007. We made so much money in 2007 that it filled in the holes left by all the previous years of loss. And then what happened in 2008?

The beginning of the economic downturn for the whole country. The construction industry in much of the country was a disaster. Nashville wasn't hit quite as hard, but it wasn't good. If that economic downturn had happened in 2005 when we were trying to get back on our feet as a company, we wouldn't have made it. By the time the downturn hit in 2008 and 2009, we were prepared for it. We were a different company. We had changed our strategy. We had changed our mix of revenues. We were much healthier.

In 2003, we were a company with way too many eggs in just a couple of baskets. I changed the structure, the composition of our revenues, to make Lee Company much more capable of enduring a financial storm, and when that storm hit, our company was prepared for it. We didn't have to shrink or lay people off. We didn't make any profit, but we didn't lose money either. We weathered the economic storm well for a construction company. Most of them took big hits. But we didn't. In part because of what happened to us in 2003 and 2004.

CHAPTER 10

THE RIPPLE EFFECT

Life is short.

So many times in life, I've remembered that scene with my dad out in the hay barn with my siblings—that day he made all of us stop and just enjoy the moment, because it was perhaps the last time we would all be together as a family working good hard honest sweaty work on the farm, stacking hay bales that later we would use to feed the cattle we were raising.

My dad was a *Life Is Short* kind of guy, and he raised a *Life Is Short* kind of son. And because I always have in the back of my mind that awareness that we have a limited amount of time on this earth, and because I always want to live the kind of life that leaves the world a better place for my having been here, and because I've grown increasingly committed to living my life purposefully and meaningfully—then if I have the opportunity to do something that might change someone's life for the better, why would I not do that? Many people would agree with me that that's worth doing, but not everyone has the capacity or the opportunity.

I have sometimes been given that opportunity.

I was introduced to Y-CAP, an at-risk youth program of the YMCA of Middle Tennessee, several years ago. I liked what I found out about the YMCA through that experience, and ended up being asked to join and eventually to chair the board.

Y-CAP has an event every year that they call *power lunch.* It involves about forty men and forty at-risk boys. (There's also one for girls—it's held on a different day.) Tables and chairs are arranged in a ring with the boys sitting on the inside and the men sitting on the outside. These are men of all types from the community—teachers, firemen, businessmen, pastors, and so on. The boys have five minutes to interview each man; every five minutes, a bell rings and they move down the circle to sit across from the next man.

In their interviews, they can ask whatever they want: "Did you go to school? For how many years? What's your job? Do you like it? Do you have a family?"

The goal of the event, of course, is to have these boys grasp something useful from that brief interaction with men from their own community who are productive, successful, contributing. Perhaps they will notice some common factors in the lives of these men, perhaps about work ethic or education. Perhaps they'll find someone whose life they'd like to emulate.

It was at a power lunch that one boy in particular sat across from me—Adam. He had a lot of questions, but one struck me: "Who inspired you most in life?"

"I'd say my father inspired me most." Then I watched him carefully and asked, "Who has inspired *you* the most?"

He stared at me for about ten seconds and shook his head. As if saying, *No, nobody really inspires me.*

And I said, "*Somebody* must have inspired you." I waited.

Again, he stared at me silently for several seconds and then just shook his head.

We moved on to his next question.

When the power lunch was over, I sought out the organizer and said, "There's a kid in your program named Adam."

He nodded. He knew who he was.

I said, "I'd like to spend more time with him."

After I went through Y-CAP's mentoring training program, a social worker introduced me to Adam and his grandmother, with whom he lived in the inner city. I would drive into his very troubled neighborhood and pick him up once a week, every week. That started five years ago. We still do it. Over those five years, we've talked about everything from faith to drugs to gangs to school to girls.

When we started, Adam was failing every class. It was clear that Adam was not being well served by the public school he was attending, and that leaving him there, far from helping him, would probably result in his getting into trouble. There were few educational choices for Adam, but I helped move him from his school to a different kind of public school, this one a charter school, where he had a completely different, and far more satisfactory, educational outcome. Observing that got me very interested in the power of public education in the life of a child—not just for Adam, but for all kids. That led me to become more involved in education reform and public education issues, including an appointment to the Tennessee Higher Education Commission.

Like so many things in my life, in mentoring Adam I have gained more than I have given. It began simply as an effort to help one child who had no one who inspired him. But it led me to get involved in education in the state in the hope of affecting other children's lives.

We never knew the impact that beginning that relationship might have on both of us, or the subsequent ripple effect that relationship might have on thousands of lives. Adam will never know, I'm sure, the positive impact that he's had—not just on me but, through my involvement in education in a way I wouldn't have pursued except for my relationship with Adam, on potentially thousands of children's lives. And that all came because of Adam's willingness to be open and transparent, and to be in a relationship with me and my wife and my family.

None of us knows the future directions Adam's life will take, of course, but it recently took a profound turn. As a high-school senior, he's being adopted by a loving family in the community. He's a remarkably gifted young man, and I eagerly anticipate seeing where his future goes.

It's very difficult for kids in the inner city to find their way out—in part because our education system has failed them. What I've learned through my relationship with Adam is that there is hope for every child, but part of that hope lies in a quality education. And because of Adam, I've become an advocate for the thousands of children who deserve that. It just makes sense. But if I hadn't gotten involved in Adam's life as a mentor, I might not have seen it as clearly as I see it now.

Many years ago, I got involved in a nonprofit called Men of Valor. It's a faith-based program in Nashville that works inside the state prison system helping men prepare for reentry into society when their sentences are up. It starts working with them about a year before they're scheduled to be released from prison, providing classes on addiction, parenting, marriage, anger management—and discipleship, since it's a faith-based organization. Then when the men are released from prison, Men of Valor helps them with transitional housing and job placement.

Men of Valor also mentors men, one on one. A lot of men on the inside have mentors on the outside, and they can continue that mentoring relationship when they're released.

When I heard about this program, it made great sense to me—something worth investing time in. So I decided to mentor a man—another Adam, coincidentally—who had already been released from prison. He and I tried to meet every week or two. Many of those meetings were at 5:00 in the morning, for an hour before he had to report to his job. Our discussions followed no curriculum, no particular program. We talked about life and hope and work and parenting. He had three children, but none of them were living with him. He was living alone.

The story of his early life wouldn't surprise you—it's similar to the story of many men in prison. When he was a child, he was mostly raised by people other than his parents. His father had never been a part of his life, and his mother had issues of her own. He spent much of his childhood in group homes. *Abandoned, neglected*—those terms may be ugly, but I think you could fairly apply them to Adam's childhood. Not surprisingly, as a young man, he self-medicated. One thing led to another, and he ended up in prison for many years for drug-related crimes.

Adam and I became good friends because of those frequent, low-pressure, casual conversations. We're still good friends today. Over the years since his release, he has regained custody of one of his children and has a relationship with another. (He has a third child, but he's unlikely to ever have a relationship with that one because he gave up parental rights long ago.) He's involved in a church and has held a steady job for many years. He's a productive citizen.

Knowing Adam has taught me that many people, given a second chance, can turn their lives around. And participating in Men of Valor has proven to me that there is a great need for effective reentry programs for men being released from prison. Only a small percentage of prison inmates die in prison—98 percent of people behind bars eventually get out of prison or jail. In my state, Tennessee, about 50 percent of those released from prison will sooner or later be sentenced again. That rate of recidivism helps no one. We need a change in how effectively we prepare inmates for reentry into society.

That concern prompted me to try to connect Men of Valor and the Department of Corrections. As a result of that effort, our governor appointed me for a year to a task force on recidivism and sentencing reform. At the end of that year, the task force recommended legislation regarding sentencing reform. The task force's job was done at that point, but our recommendations are still in effect.

My experience with Adam prompted me to continue to connect with men in prison. I have heard their personal stories, and I have been touched by them. Am I getting soft on crime? No—I believe that those who do the crime should do the time, that we should be tough on crime *when it's appropriate.* Violent criminals, repeat offenders—there are certainly men in prison who should be kept there for a long, long time. Yes, I'm tough on crime.

But...

There is a way to be tough on crime and *smart* on crime at the same time. Nearly all of the men currently behind bars in our state and every other will get out sometime. It would be smart for us to look at how we can influence and educate them in ways that make it less likely they'll be back. Why? Because if they do end up being convicted and sentenced again, that means there's been another crime committed, and that means another victim. In addition to the personal cost to the victim and the victim's family, there's a dollar cost to taxpayers. In Tennessee, that cost is currently about $30,000 a year for every inmate in every state prison. In some states it's much higher— New York pays twice that figure.

Yes, I'm tough on crime, but getting to know Adam and working within a broken criminal justice system taught me that it's about more than being tough. It's about being smart too, and sometimes that means extending mercy.

Talking to so many men in prison has underlined the truth of something I already suspected: If I'd had their personal stories as a child—if I'd grown up like Adam—I might be in prison too. I'm continually astonished at the consistency of their stories of brutal childhoods, of the things that happened to them when they were four, or five, or six, or seven that most of us can't imagine. I'm amazed at their stories of being exposed to, of witnessing, things no young child should ever see or hear or experience.

Even kids who are adopted out of a difficult childhood like that and given a place in a productive and loving family may still, if the adoption takes place when they are five, six, seven years old or older, have some of those patterns so engrained in their psyches that they will have the same struggles in adolescence and adulthood they would have had if they had remained in their original home.

Does that eliminate or reduce their guilt for the crimes they've committed, for the people they've hurt? No. People still need to pay for their crimes, regardless of how poorly they were treated as children. But it does make us realize that the world of crime and its causation is more complex than we may have thought. It makes me believe all the more that appropriate preparation for reentry is critical.

I decided years ago that part of the call on my life is to expand my impact by becoming involved in nonprofits in my community and in other parts of the world. And what I discovered on my first effort to serve in this way, my first mission trip (to Mexico), was that I was by far the greatest beneficiary of that experience, not those I had gone to serve. The next time I had an opportunity to serve through a nonprofit, I went not only because it might help others but because it would enrich my own life just as much, if not more. It is indeed more blessed to give than to receive. This truly is what brings fulfillment.

And that's why I've participated in missions trips to Mexico, Haiti, Africa, and Iraq. I've served with organizations such as a homeless shelter, a women's health clinic, and inner-city at-risk youth programs.

I've chosen to share these two particular examples, the stories of the Adams in my life, because they are for me a reflection of the profound ripple effect of serving. They illustrate that lives of service are lives well lived. That loving your neighbor as yourself really does sum up what Christianity should be. And that those who sow reap a far more rewarding harvest than they imagined—not only for themselves, but sometimes for thousands or even millions.

CHAPTER 11

Miss D

For the first year or two after losing Carol Ann, my days and nights were mostly taken up with being the parent of four grieving kids, as well as with finding ways to navigate my way through my own grief. And then came Jessica's suicide attempt and the attention that required from me. What little time and energy I had for social interaction was spent either providing fun activities for the kids or with one of my buddies, eating out or going to the gym or the movies.

A lot of single guys my age would have been dating. At first, I didn't have the energy or the emotional bandwidth even to consider it. Besides, I didn't want my children to go through another trauma. And I knew that my getting married would be tough for them no matter who I married, at least within the first five years or so of losing their mom. I was determined not to put my kids through something like that. I didn't need to get married, and I simply wouldn't. It was a conscious decision.

Caleb and Jacob, being twins, were in the third grade at the same time, but in different classes. Maria DiNenna was Caleb's teacher. Carol Ann and I went to the open house at the beginning of the year and met the teachers. As we drove home, Carol Ann and I shared our mutually positive response to Maria: "She's a really nice girl. I like her a lot." And she *did* seem young enough to call a girl. Obviously, she was old enough to have graduated from college and gotten a teaching job. But she was ten years younger than me, and I still thought of myself as pretty young.

Poor Caleb—he had quite a crush on Maria, and the rest of us teased him about it unmercifully. He wrote her notes and painted pictures for her, and he talked about her constantly

He would come down to breakfast in one shirt, then before leaving for school would change into a different one. "What happened to the red shirt?" we would ask.

"I don't think Miss D liked it when I wore it before," he would respond.

"Honey, Miss D doesn't care what you wear," Carol Ann would say. But it didn't matter—he would continue to choose his clothes based on which he thought she would like most.

The summer after the boys' third-grade year was the summer everything changed for us. Carol Ann's death left each of us reeling. Nine-year-old Caleb, like all of us, needed to talk to someone about it—and who did he call? Miss D.

They talked on the phone for an hour. She was his closest confidante.

I worried about how the kids would do in returning to school that fall, but I was reassured by one thing: Miss D had decided to move from third grade to fourth grade. I asked the principal, "Can I put both of the boys in Miss DiNenna's class?" I didn't know that Maria, having made such a strong connection with Caleb in the third grade, had already talked to the principal about putting both boys in her fourth-grade class so that, at such a difficult time for our family, I wouldn't have to deal with two teachers. It was the first time the boys would be in the same class since they began school.

So she had both boys, Caleb and Jacob, in fourth grade, starting just weeks after their mother's death.

Since I was their only parent that year, I was very involved in my kids' schooling and knew their teachers. So Maria and I got to know each other well, and I began to realize just how special this "girl" was. Miss D was one of the favorite teachers at school. At any school function kids would surround her, and her love for them was evident as well. But she was also loved and respected by the parents, not just because she was a great teacher but because she was a great person with a big heart, a beautiful smile, and a unique quality that reassured you that she was someone you could trust. In fact, she came to the house and watched the kids for me a few times when I had to be out of town—something she'd done for Carol Ann and me a few times the previous year, too, and that she did for the families of other students. She was a single teacher people liked and trusted and their kids loved her, so it seemed natural. All of my kids became close to her, and she to them.

After about two years of that, Maria and I started to look at each other differently. And I can remember the night it began. It was a school event, and I was there because my kids were involved. As the time approached for the event to start, I noticed Maria, the teacher, on the stage—reassuring frightened kids, helping them all find their places, acting with confidence and compassion and competence—and I admired what she was doing. But I had to be honest: I wasn't just admiring her competence, I was also appreciating her beauty. *She's a bunch of years younger than you,* I reminded myself. *Isn't it a little weird to find yourself attracted to a woman that much younger? And your kids' teacher to boot?*

Weird or not, I began to think that there were possibilities there for romance. I talked with my kids about it and, with their blessing, I suggested to Maria that we change the footing of our relationship—that we try dating and see how it goes.

So we went out to dinner—but mostly our "trying out dating" consisted of talking on the phone. It lasted two or three weeks—two or three weeks during which I was becoming progressively less comfortable with that arrangement, on all fronts: *I'm not ready for this,* I thought. *It's not going to work. I don't think she's the right person. It feels wrong. It's just too soon.* And it *was* too soon—for me, at least. I was still grieving the loss of Carol Ann, whom I had adored, and about whose death I was still devastated.

Definitely too soon.

So I called Maria and said, "I can't do this now. Let's not see each other romantically any more. We can still be friends, of course, but we're not dating."

To say that was hard for Maria would be an understatement. It was terrible for her. She had really begun to invest herself in the idea that there was a future for the six of us as a family unit, and now I was taking that future off the table. At the time I didn't understand the depth of her anguish over it, but maybe that was because I was thinking, *Okay, we've been dating for three weeks. It's not working out, so let's end it now before somebody gets hurt.* But for Maria, it hadn't been just three weeks—she had been investing a lot of emotion in the kids for much longer than that. Because of her frequent times staying with the kids in our house, it had begun to feel like home to her. Not just the house—the relationships with the kids as well. And I had just taken all of that away from her.

For a while after we ended the dating part of our relationship, Maria and I kept our friendship alive and she still came to babysit the kids. But once I began to date other women, things became awkward between us and she said, "I can't keep your kids anymore. It's getting too complicated, too hard—your feelings have changed, but mine haven't. I think it's best if we just don't see each other outside of school."

For the next three or four years, I dated quite a bit. I dated one woman for a couple of years. But I never really got Maria out of my mind, and on those frequent occasions when we would run into each other, mostly at school events, I very much enjoyed seeing her. Occasionally I would wonder—did I bail out on our relationship too soon, too easily? Or, given that I had concluded, probably correctly, that it had been too soon for me to be dating again, should we give it another try now that more time had passed? Each time I thought that, though, I came back to the same idea: We had given it a few weeks and it hadn't seemed to be working. Breaking it off had caused Maria a lot of emotional pain. If we tried it again and then I decided that I'd been right the first time and that she wasn't the right one and we should break it off again, she would be hurt even worse. So I thought, *I can't go there even if want to. If we broke up a second time, it would be terrible. I can't do that to her. When I feel that old attraction to Maria, I'll just ignore it.*

So I dated someone else. And someone else. And someone else. And none of those relationships worked out. Not because there was anything wrong with the women I was dating—they were wonderful ladies—but somehow they never seemed to be someone I would want to spend the rest of my life with. And then I would go to one of the kids' school events and we would see Maria there, and my heart would quicken not just with chemistry but with a genuine fondness. I was always happy to see her in a way that didn't seem to be true with the other women I dated. I found myself thinking about her more and more.

I was constantly running into her. Constantly. I would see her in her classroom as I would walk past, and I would wave. I would see her at a track meet and wave. I would see her at a basketball game and she would wave at me. And each time it was like dropping a grain of sand on the balancing tray of a scale. One grain of sand made no difference. And the next time, another grain of sand—but again, just one more was too light to unbalance the scale of equilibrium. After a few years of adding a grain of sand to the scale each time I saw her, eventually the point came where that last grain of sand became the added weight that upset the equilibrium and the scale tipped. And when that happened I could no longer ignore it, and I thought, *It's time to revisit this.*

I prayed about it. I talked to my buddy Lynn about it—the close friend I hung out with every week. "What am I supposed to do about this?" I asked him. "I'm beginning to think that this really *is* what God has in mind for me, and if that's true, then it's what he has in mind for Maria too. But I'm just not yet sure. And if I'm wrong—I just don't want to hurt her again."

If it seems like I was being a little too cautious here—why not just date her again for a few months and see?—remember that I had a history of getting cold feet. I had been in an agony over my upcoming wedding when Carol Ann and I were engaged the first time, to the extent that we called it off and were apart for two long years. And I had already broken off my romantic connection with Maria once. So I had a legitimate fear: No matter how wonderful Maria is, will I be able to hold up my end of the deal without freaking out when we start getting too close?

My kids knew her and loved her—but even that was becoming less of an issue. By this time, Jessica was in college and the boys in high school. The kids, I realized, would probably be fine with it if I got married, and if issues arose, they would adjust.

The kids knew, of course, that I'd been dating for some time. But they didn't know the women—I never brought them home. Whether that was a good decision or not, I just didn't want my kids to be part of it until I started to get serious about somebody.

Eventually, I felt sure that Maria was the right one for me—and that, in fact, she always had been and I just hadn't been able to see it. When I felt sure that I would be able to be fair and stable with her in a romantic relationship, it was time to talk to her about it.

I ran into her at school the first day of the 2007–08 school year and said that I'd like to see the pictures she'd taken on a mission trip to Guatemala she'd just returned from. It took me a few nervous weeks to make good on that and invite her out to the house for dinner. That night I didn't even look at the pictures she had brought that I'd said I wanted to see. Instead, I said, "What would you think about the two of us dating again? Shall we give it a try—maybe go out for dinner one night soon? We can look at the pictures from your trip afterward."

If I'd been expecting her to jump at the opportunity, I was surprised at her initial reluctance. She said she'd have to think about it. She called up her friends and asked what they thought—and they all advised her strongly against it! They must not have thought I could be trusted to be careful with her heart.

Eventually, though, she agreed. For our first date, since Maria's family is Italian, we went to an Italian restaurant.

There was a second date, and a third, and soon we were dating regularly.

We dated through the winter, and it didn't take us long to realize where our relationship was heading. But how should we tell the kids? And when would be the best time? At first we thought, *Let's just wait until the boys go off to college—then we'll get married.* And then we decided, *No, let's get married before they leave home—that way they won't come home from college to a different situation than they left.*

So we got engaged in June and set a wedding date for October of the boys' senior year.

CHAPTER 12

AFRICA

As Maria and I made plans for our wedding in the fall, there was something else I was planning—something I had been talking about for a long time.

When my first wife, Carol Ann, died, we had asked people to contribute, in lieu of flowers or other ways to memorialize her life, to a fund we created called the Carol Ann Lee Memorial Fund that would be used for charitable gifts in her memory. We were now ready to make the first gift from that fund. A friend, Larry Warren, served in Africa with an organization called African Leadership, and the kids and I had agreed that the first gift from the fund would be to finance a project there. But we didn't yet know what project we would fund. The five of us, the four kids and I, planned to make a trip to Africa ourselves to inspect several sites with projects that needed funding and choose one of them. From my perspective as a father, I saw this as a priceless opportunity not just to see a brand-new part of the world, enjoy some recreation with my kids and expand their horizons, but also to give them a firsthand opportunity to learn about and experience the joy of generosity.

And the time to do it was now. With the kids' school situation getting more diverse—Jessica was already in college, and Jacob and Caleb would start college after the next school year—we feared that things might get too complicated between school and jobs, and that if we didn't do it now we never would.

Making the moment especially bittersweet for me, I suspected that this would be the last time all four of the kids and I would have the chance to vacation together. I had concluded by that time, and still believe, that life comes packaged in seasons. And this trip would mark the end of that particular season.

Life starts with the season of childhood. Then adolescence. Then, at least for me, the first season of marriage, when it was just me and my wife and no kids. Next comes the season of marriage that includes young kids and all of the challenges of raising them. Sadly for the Lee family, that was a too-short season, followed by the season of single-parenting, just me and the four kids. I say *sadly* for us because the circumstances that ushered in that season were clearly unfortunate, but the season itself was bittersweet—given the closeness the four kids and I experienced during those years. A season like that is not something anyone plans on or desires, but we weren't given a choice. We lived through it with commitment and love for each other, and I have many wonderful memories of those years. It started bitter and it ended sweet. During those years I grew closer to my kids, and they to me, than I could ever have imagined—not *despite* but rather *because* of the loss that had ushered those years into our lives. By the end of that season, marked by the departure of the kids for college, we were a remarkably rich, deep, full, wonderful family, each member of which was growing and succeeding in ways I could never have predicted.

This trip would put a period at the end of that season.

When my kids were younger, we had always done a lot of mission work—in Appalachia before the kids were old enough for international travel, and then in Mexico with Youth With a Mission to help build houses for the poor. But this trip would be unique. This time, all four of my children were old enough to really appreciate and understand not only the needs we were attempting to meet but to participate in the decision of just how to express generosity together.

The flight to Africa—a big deal and exciting for all of us— took well over thirty hours and took us through New York and London on our way to Nairobi. Larry, who lived close to us in Franklin, Tennessee, had planned and organized our trip for us. He'd lived in Africa off and on for many years.

We visited three different works that Larry's organization had been involved in in Kenya and Uganda. One was a school for disadvantaged children. One was a church in the middle of a slum in Nairobi, Kenya's capital city. That church had a great ministry serving the poorest of the poor in one of the worst and most poverty-stricken neighborhoods on the entire globe. And one of the sites was in northern Uganda, just below the Sudanese border in a town called Gulu which had recently been featured in a story about the "invisible children." We would visit a ministry there that assisted refugees.

We flew first to Nairobi and spent three or four days visiting the school and the church that provided services to the poverty stricken. But before we flew on to Gulu, I thought, *Who knows—neither I nor the kids may ever get the chance to visit Africa again. Let's take advantage of this opportunity to do and see things we can't anywhere else.* So we hopped a ride on a plane into the Masai Mara, a region of Africa known for safaris into its wide-open plains. We spent a couple of days there on a photographic safari, sleeping in tents and riding Range Rovers across the countryside. We saw every form of wildlife imaginable in that part of the region: giraffes, elephants, lions, leopards, crocodiles, zebras, and more—animals that I'd never seen except in movies, television, or in zoos, and here they were in the wild. What an experience to be able to give my kids! Even though the purpose of our trip was serious and came in response to desperate need, the trip also provided beauty in the midst of squalor.

And the beauty provided a unique backdrop to the poverty and the emotional and physical damage we were about to see in Gulu.

Joseph Kony, the ruthless dictator in Sudan, was slaughtering the people of Sudan by the tens of thousands. He would kill parents and abduct their children. The boys he would turn into soldiers, and the captured girls were turned over to the male soldiers to use however they wished. They called the girls "child mothers."

There were huge groups of boy soldiers and child mothers all through southern Sudan. Many of them escaped and fled south to the refugee camps of Northern Uganda, some of which had tens of thousands of people in them. Other children in those camps had never been captured by Kony or his forces but had been sent there by Sudanese parents who hoped their children could avoid the destruction and terror of the Kony regime.

The ministry we were to visit in Gulu was providing services for former child mothers and boy soldiers, some of whom were now young adults and living with the psychological and physical aftermath of that trauma.

We caught a commercial flight from Nairobi to Entebbe, where we boarded a small plane operated by MAF—Mission Aviation Fellowship. There were eight of us on the flight—the five of us Lees, the pilot, our friend Larry who had arranged the trip, and Kristen, Jessica's best friend who often vacationed with us. That flight was fascinating for a number of reasons. At one point, Jacob yelled up to the pilot, "What river is that?"

The pilot turned around and yelled, "It's the Nile!"

This trip was full of moments like that, when we realized that we were somewhere we had heard of all our lives, and we found it, like the entire continent, to be vast and awe-inspiring.

The further north we flew into Uganda, the more rural society became. When we looked down, we gradually noticed that rather than seeing buildings and rooftops, we were seeing the round, grass-topped roofs of villages full of huts, and on the dirt roads, occasional women—topless and wearing long skirts—walking with baskets or pots balanced on their heads. *Wow*, I thought. *This is Africa.* We had already been in Africa for four or five days, but what we were seeing now was a whole new kind of Africa.

We checked into a hotel in Gulu. Bear in mind that hotels in a poor area like this are not like checking into Courtyard by Marriott. Our hotel had a community bath. It had a bathtub but no shower, so you just poured pitchers of water over yourself while you sat in a tub.

Every night at about 10:00, big, steel, barred doors would be locked over the hotel entrance so that no one could come into the facility during the night. We were instructed to not open the doors during the evening hours even to go from one room to the next because it wasn't safe to leave your room at night.

Just one of many things that reminded us we weren't in America anymore.

In Gulu, we spent five of the most eye-opening, phenomenal days of our lives:

- Touring a refugee camp.
- Praying with people—mostly people who didn't speak English, but we were accompanied everywhere by interpreters supplied by the mission.
- Visiting an orphanage.
- Worshipping with a group of AIDs patients.

- Touring what they call a hospital, but it felt to us more like a barn or, at best, an army field hospital in a combat zone: primitive, open air, characterized by rows and rows of beds crammed side by side and a serious lack of equipment and medication.
- Walking through tuberculosis wards.

It was overwhelming. We saw so much every day that by dinnertime we were on complete emotional and informational overload. Every night we would sit and process—what we'd seen, what we'd experienced, what we felt about it, how we thought it would shape who we were in the future. Larry would sit and process with us.

It was a powerful, impactful trip, but not a safe one. This was in 2008, and while the circumstances in northern Uganda had improved, it still couldn't be described as safe. Long before we left the US, my kids and I had discussed the level of danger and they wanted to go anyway, despite the risk. In fact, that seemed to make the trip even more meaningful for them. We were risking our own safety to do something good for someone else.

The morning before we were to leave Gulu, my kids and I walked the streets and found a little breakfast spot, a street café. Describing it like that makes it sound like the sort of delightful little place you might find on the sidewalks of Paris, or like the chairs and umbrellas outside a Panera Bread. But it was nothing like that. It was not a *sidewalk* café, because there were no sidewalks. There were cheap plastic chairs and little metal tables placed right along the edge of the road, and just an arm's length away from us as we ate were children walking down the dirt street on their way to school.

There is a beautiful and wonderful way about Africa that, once you've been there, is etched into your mind forever. Particularly when you know that you'll fly back home to all that America holds—an abundance and overflow—when the children who walked past our café table had too little, by far.

No, definitely not Panera. Not worse—just different.

For one thing, the food. Throughout our African trip, we were very careful about what we ordered and what we ate. But in many ways, you have little choice. When you're in a remote region like that, you either eat what's available or you eat nothing. We all assumed that we would get sick from the food, and we had brought medicine for it. And of course, we were right—every single one of us was terribly sick at least one day. We would laugh about it, trying to predict who was next and when. We each ended up once having to spend at least half the day in the hotel room.

Most places where we ate served eggs, and eggs were reasonably safe. We tried to stay away from the meat. We tried to stay away from the vegetables. But you can't stay away from everything—especially since most of what they served was some kind of stew—a pot of food with everything in it. So you finally just give in and eat. And afterwards pay for it with something like food poisoning.

As simple and poverty-stricken and dirty as that café was, it was a beautiful place for us to make our decision. So we ordered our food and sat together, I and my four kids, and talked about all we'd seen over the last ten or twelve days. What things had been the most meaningful and most poignant to us? Where did we believe that our gift would make the most difference?

We had lots of ideas, and I was pleased with the compassion and creativity I was hearing from Jessica, Jacob, Caleb, and Sarah Kate. In the end, one need stood out to us more than the others. The child mothers were cared for at that ministry compound only until they reached the age of sixteen, because there just wasn't room for them there after that. So at sixteen, those girls were released. Just released—to go out on the street and make their own way in life, with little in the way of help or support and no place to live. After everything that had happened to them in life up to that point, and even though they had been helped through childhood, it just didn't seem to us that they were ready yet to be out on their own. I realize that it's a poor comparison, but I found myself thinking of how girls in the States would fare if they were turned out onto the streets right after their sixteenth birthday.

So we chose to fund a building to provide housing for those teenage child mothers so that they wouldn't have to leave the compound quite yet. The funds that we designated for the project were enough to build the entire facility, and we dedicated it to the memory of Carol Ann.

We left that day on the forty-hour journey back to Nashville. Gulu to Entebbe, where we had a long layover. Entebbe to Nairobi. Nairobi to Frankfurt. Frankfurt to Chicago. Chicago to home.

Oddly, one of the experiences in Africa that typifies for me the lifestyle of those who live there, especially in comparison with the way we live in America, was our visit to the marketplace in Gulu. If you were to try to find something comparable in the US, you'd have to look at farmers' markets, but that's not an accurate comparison, except for the fact that at a farmers' market you have a collection of independent vendors who themselves produced the food they're selling, as in Gulu. The marketplace in Gulu was filled with a wide variety of foods of varying quality: fish, various mostly unidentifiable animal carcasses hanging upside down by their feet, and a huge variety of vegetables, many of which I didn't recognize. And chickens—chickens everywhere: killed and plucked, or living and confined to boxes or crates, or bound by their feet to keep them from escaping, and their clucks and squawks and crows filled the air. If there was one sound more inescapable than the sound of the chickens, and if there was one animal more numerous, it was flies. Seemingly every surface, especially the surface of any meat or fish left in the open, was covered by flies. Add to that the smells, some wonderfully fragrant and others that made you cover your nose with your hand, and the color-ful, energetic personalities of the vendors and the consumers, people who make you want to grab your camera to help retain the memory—in fact, the whole experience seemed like some-thing you would see on the pages of *National Geographic*.

My description of Gulu, I realize, sounds mostly terrible. Never before had we realized just what privilege and plenty we in America live in. When you're surrounded by, and meet and speak with, people who struggle each day simply to achieve the basic requirements of life, you're both appreciative of how Americans live and also humbled. The level of poverty we saw in Gulu is really how most people in the world live.

And yet—do I pity them? They could certainly use some help with food, shelter, medical supplies—frankly, by the standards of the western world, their existence is miserable. Few people would choose to live like the poor of Gulu—not that those who live in those conditions do so by choice. But what's the abiding mental image I have of the people there? It's of their smiling faces, of their joy, their playfulness. They rise above their circumstances. They enjoy each other. They enjoy life. They laugh, they smile, they dance even in their worship. Their children are as happy, active, and playful as children anywhere. We can learn something from the poor of Gulu, and there's much to be said for achieving a more simple life than most of us live in the US.

In truth, I would love to go back for a visit right now.

The trip sparked a love of missions in my kids. After Africa, all six of us, including Maria, went to Mexico to help build houses for those who can't afford it on their own. Sarah Kate, Maria, and I went together to Haiti to work in an orphanage. Jacob was the one of the four who most powerfully caught the vision for missions. He has traveled to missions projects in China, South Africa, and India.

The Africa trip proved life-changing not just for Jacob but for all five of us—and for the young women who had a place to live, thanks to a gift from the Carol Ann Lee Memorial Fund, a fund set up half a world away to memorialize an unforgettable woman dedicated to generosity and compassion.

CHAPTER 13

MARRYING MARIA

In October 2008, Maria and I married.

Over the years that Maria and I had known each other, even when we weren't dating, she still had a close and affectionate relationship with the rest of my family—not just the boys, having been their schoolteacher, and Jessica, having been her cross-country and track coach, and Sarah Kate, having watched over her along with the rest of them when I was away, but with my parents and siblings as well. She was a familiar figure around the farm.

Every year we would have a cattle sale, and my dad, who thought Maria was delightful, would ask her to come during the sale to help with the food. Even when things had been awkward between Maria and me, her relationship with the rest of my extended family had been warm and relaxed.

So when we decided to get married, we agreed that getting married on the farm was the right choice. But I was particularly concerned that it be what Maria wanted. This would be her first wedding, and I wanted it to be exactly as she would like it to be.

She had always wanted a wedding in October, when the leaves were beautiful, so that's how we set the date. We planned to have it outside, along a creek at the edge of a pasture—a beautiful spot just down the road from what was soon to be *our* house. We decided to have the reception right there on the farm as well, in a big tent in the pasture a short walk from the wedding site. A beautiful place.

It was a big wedding—we invited everyone that the two of us knew together. Maria had lived in middle Tennessee for fourteen years and I was born and raised there, so we had a lot of friends. And it has been an incredible gift to me, to us both, the extent to which Maria's friends have become my friends and my friends have become Maria's friends. The melding of our lives over the years seems in many ways seamless, and that's especially true with regard to friendships. As a couple, Maria and I have been able to maintain all the friendships that each of us had as single adults. And any friends of mine who had been friends with Carol Ann and I as a couple have enfolded Maria into their midst with love and great openness. For instance, there was a prayer group that Debbie and Michael W. Smith and Carol Ann and I were involved in back before Carol Ann and I were even married and then throughout our marriage. The women from that prayer group began meeting regularly as well, not just for prayer but to socialize. Once Maria and I married, the women of that prayer group reached out to her and brought her in, and to this day she meets with those women every week.

Most of those friends were there for our wedding, all of them delighted that we had found each other. Maria's friends were happy that she had found someone to share the rest of her life with. My friends were grateful that I had healed enough over the past several years that I was capable, once again, of having a relationship like this. It was a joyful occasion not only for us but for the people who were there. All of us saw it as a story of redemption—an example of how God works in really tough circumstances to bring together a beautiful ending.

Out of the bitter, he made something sweet.

The wedding was just as we'd planned it, with just the flowers she wanted and just the food we'd chosen. The band was made up of gifted musicians who were good friends of ours. The wedding was simple and beautiful. My best friend Lynn, along with my brother and my sons, were in the wedding. My daughters and Maria's sisters and two of her closest friends were in the wedding. Her brother read scripture, and her nieces and nephews were flower girls and ring bearers and ushers. Maria wore a flowing wedding gown, and her mother sat watching as her father walked her across the green field on a crisp fall day, a picture I will never forget.

It was exactly the way it should be.

And when it got dark enough—fireworks! This was a surprise Maria had planned that I'd known nothing about. Maria loves fireworks. On the Fourth of July, her favorite holiday of the year, she's like a little kid. Loads of people stayed late into the evening with music, drink, and food.

I kissed my kids goodbye and Maria and I headed to downtown Nashville for our wedding night in the historic Union Station Hotel. In the morning, we boarded a plane for the British Virgin Islands.

It struck me as our plane took off that morning that I had not taken a vacation to do the things that I wanted to do in a place I chose for myself in a very, very long time. So it was especially gratifying to arrive in the Virgin Islands that day and check into a beautiful, historic resort right on the water.

Even though we wanted to do as little as possible but relax, enjoy the tropical beauty, and enjoy each other as well, we didn't want to completely ignore the opportunities of being in the Caribbean. One day we went for a long hike along the ridge of the island and climbed down into a little cove with a deserted, romantic beach where we spent a few hours completely by ourselves. We took a sunset cruise on a sailboat to some of the adjoining islands one afternoon and evening and had dinner on one of the islands. On the return trip, the cool breeze, having Maria in my arms, and watching the moonlight dancing on the water was like a scene out of a movie. We spent part of a day snorkeling—and the snorkeling is astonishing in the Virgin Islands; we saw incredible fish and other creatures. Most nights we ate at a great restaurant out on the sand. We'd sit and drink wine and eat dinner and listen to the live music from the steel-drum band.

It was just perfect—a very small resort with few guests. For the entire week we slept late, read, ate, and lay on the beach.

After our return flight landed in Nashville, we spent the night downtown again, just to get ready for reentry. And then we went home on Sunday.

On Monday morning, of course, there was school for the kids. Maria and I were lying in bed that morning, having been married only a week and after our first night at home. We had just awakened and were about to get out of bed. Suddenly Jacob walked into the bedroom.

Apparently I had forgotten to mention to Maria that the master bath was also Jacob's shower room in the morning, and had been for a couple of years. Jacob and Caleb shared a bathroom, and to make sure everyone was able to get ready for the day without any unpleasant juggling of schedules, Caleb showered in their bathroom and Jacob showered in mine. Only it was no longer just mine—now it was mine and Maria's, and she didn't consider that to be a pleasant surprise. She wasn't able to do more than stammer as he walked through the room, waved at us, and continued into the bathroom, where he turned on the shower.

Then she found her voice. "What was that?"

So I explained. It seemed perfectly normal to me—a good solution to the age-old problem of a house full of teenagers and a limited number of showers. It didn't seem very normal to her that a teenage boy would wander through her bedroom every morning.

That was the first of a number of intense conversations we had around that situation and others. It was a challenging transition for all of us. I hadn't adequately considered what accommodation the rest of us might need to make to having Maria living among us.

She was thirty-nine. She had never been married and, other than her nieces and nephews and the students she taught every day who loved her and whom she loved, she had no children.

She had grown up in a modest home in a middle-class neighborhood with a stay-at-home mom and a hardworking dad. His grandparents had been immigrants from Italy, and from his father he had learned the skilled trade of laying tile. He had worked on his knees his whole life.

Having been single for her entire adult life up to that point, she had made a life for herself. She had a group of friends and a life she enjoyed as a schoolteacher. She lived in a little house she and a friend had bought together since neither of them could afford one on their own.

At least all of that had been her life until we married, and then suddenly she was part of my world—married to the CEO of a company that employed several hundred people—not tile layers like her dad but hardworking people even so: plumbers, electricians, heating and air conditioning specialists. Now, suddenly, she had four kids. Now, suddenly, she lived on a big farm that my family owned and had extended family all over the place.

Maria had just jumped onto a fast-moving train.

For her, everything had changed. Everything. But nothing much had changed for me. The hardest parts of the transition were hers. And yes, she did feel the injustice of that.

Of course, the kids and I did have *some* changes to make. When you've lived eight years on your own, making every decision without the need to consult anybody about anything, going where you want, when you want—it can be jarring to suddenly have to share that decision-making prerogative with someone else. Jarring—but wonderful, too. I had been lonely. Years before I had decided that since I didn't *need* to have a mate, for the sake of the kids I wouldn't. But not *needing* someone to share life with is not the same thing as not *wanting* someone. And finally I had that someone.

There's a certain awkwardness to falling in love so late in life, and (in my case at least) after a first marriage. It feels so much more natural—and traditional—to fall in love as young people and then create a life together. When life develops that way, everything that happens—buying a house, having a baby, making career choices—is happening for the first time for both of you, and you're experiencing it together. That's not true when you're going through it in your forties or fifties. To my shame, there's so much about Maria—about who she is, about what makes her unique—that I didn't understand or appreciate until after we were married. Yes, life was busy when Maria and I were courting—I had kids at home and I was running a company and had many other demands on my time. We went out on dates, we had activities with the kids, but we didn't have large blocks of time alone as most couples do before they have children. The opportunity for us to be alone together was rare. Because of that, I didn't know what a gift I had received until well after I'd received it. I didn't realize how alone and empty my emotional and social life had been until we married and I realized that, for the first time in many, many years, I felt completed.

Maria has a unique way of making people feel comfortable no matter who they are. She makes the people around her feel welcomed, loved, and appreciated. She pulls people in, and that graciousness causes people to be attracted to her. I've heard it said that there are two kinds of people: the "Here I am!" person, who always wants people to notice him, who wants to be at the center of every social event, and the "*There* you are!" person, who always puts the spotlight on others and makes them feel valued and appreciated. Maria is definitely a "*There* you are!" person.

Maria has a servant's heart. She's committed to serving people through words and deeds. She's the first to make a meal for people in times of need. Or clean their house. Or offer a ride. When she senses that someone's down, she writes cards.

Now that my grandchildren have begun to arrive—five so far!—which I consider a wonderful blessing, I can say that having Maria as my wife makes having grandchildren even more wonderful. She's ten years younger than me, and therefore young to be a grandmother, but she makes a wonderful one regardless. To the grandkids she's *Eeya*, undoubtedly a shortened version of Maria, and I'm *Beebee*. To some it might feel as if Maria's place in our family is fairly recent—but to the grand-kids, she's just part of the family structure they were born into. She's their Eeya, no ifs ands or buts, and they adore her as she adores them.

The Lord knew exactly what he was doing when he brought me Maria. She was exactly the person that I needed, in ways that become ever increasingly clear to me as our life contin-ues. And I like to think, too, that God chose me especially for Maria, and that my contribution to her life is as substantial, as indispensable as hers to mine.

CHAPTER 14

THE VIEW FROM THE TOP

I saw the Tetons for the first time in my life when I was eighteen years old. My father took my brother and me on a hunting trip to the Yukon Territory, near Alaska. We drove the whole way in our pickup, and halfway there we passed through Yellowstone National Park and Grand Teton National Park. I was awestruck. I fell in love, and I've been in love with that area of the country ever since.

The first couple of times I saw the Tetons, I thought, *Wouldn't it be cool to actually climb the Grand Teton?* It's the highest peak in the entire Teton Range at almost 14,000 feet. But there were always so many other remarkable things to do in life, so many great places to go, that climbing the Grand Teton never quite made it to the top of the list. And the older I got, the less likely it was to ever happen.

When Jessica was about twelve, our whole family went on a weekend trip to Chattanooga where we saw a 3-D IMAX movie called *Everest*. She walked out of *Everest* and said, with all the unrealistic enthusiasm of a twelve year old, "I want to climb Mount Everest someday!"

"Everest?" I said. "Not me—too hard, too cold, and too dangerous. But there's something we *can* do someday—there's a mountain in Wyoming called the Grand Teton. It's not as high as Everest, but it's still very high—way above timberline and far above anything else close to it. We can climb that one someday."

I doubt that either of us gave the idea another thought until Jessica's sixteenth birthday was approaching. Those few months since her suicide attempt had undoubtedly been the most unique period of time in our relationship before or since. During her recovery, we talked often and at great depth about what had happened and what it meant in our lives. We talked about where our lives were headed. I was constantly checking with her about how she was feeling about life and how she felt she was progressing.

The closer her birthday came, the more I found myself wanting to do something with her, just the two of us, to celebrate her continuing progress. Something to mark the beginning of a new season in both our lives. "Why don't we go on a trip of some kind?" I suggested. "Someplace unique."

And then I remembered that conversation after we saw *Everest.* "Let's climb the Grand, Jessica," I said. "As your birthday present and as a special celebration."

She wasn't twelve years old any longer, and I don't think the idea initially sounded so great to her. Her response was something like, "Whatever, Dad. Okay." But she was determined to get back to a healthy and self-sufficient place in life and therefore willing to do whatever I thought was best for her healing. She was willing to take advice from me and from her counselor. So the Grand Teton climbing trip got inked onto our calendars.

That actually started a tradition in our family: taking each of my kids for a one-on-one trip with Dad on their sixteenth birthday. For the boys, it was snow-skiing trips, and with Sarah Kate a scuba-diving expedition. But it started with Jessica and the Grand Teton.

You don't embark on a challenging expedition like that without training first. We spent weeks getting into shape. Or at least I did. I'd always kept active and used the gym regularly, but climbing a mountain of nearly 14,000 feet requires a whole different kind of conditioning. Jessica already had a head start on me as an athlete, having been a member of the state champion 4 x 800 meter relay team and second in the state in women's pole vault. She'd spent all of her almost sixteen years living in the country and out in the woods, so the idea of climbing the Grand Teton didn't intimidate her. It intimidated me a whole lot more, not only because of the physical exertion but also because it sounded dangerous.

Together we read books about the Tetons. We decided together which mountain guide company we would use. We determined the route we would climb. And then we read everything we could find about the route—specific details about the climb. We researched the equipment we would need.

When we flew into Jackson Hole and met our guide (from Exum Mountain Guides), the physical conditioning continued—we had to qualify to do the climb. Not to mention getting acclimated to the elevation. Jackson Hole itself is over 6,000 feet in elevation, and we would be climbing to nearly 14,000 feet. They don't want to take up the mountain someone who's going to have to be carried back down because he just isn't in good enough shape or doesn't know enough about climbing.

We went to a mountain climbing outfitter in Jackson Hole and got the equipment we needed—the right shoes, the right ropes, the right harness and helmets. This is a technical climb. It's not a hike. Those of you who aren't experienced climbers, envision some scene from a mountain-climbing movie you've seen—recall the sight of a climber on a nearly vertical rock cliff face, attached to and suspended from a thin rope, wearing a helmet and with a collection of shiny carabiners and chocks attached to a ring on his belt. That's the type of climbing we would be doing. Neither of us had ever done it before, so we would be dependent on the leadership of our guide.

Exum handled the training and conditioning by taking us out for two days in the foothills at the base of the Teton Range, going over climbing technique and making sure we knew the terms that we would soon be yelling out to one another. This type of climbing is a team effort but when you climb, you aren't arm's length from each other. There'll be some distance, and you'll have to yell down an instruction to the one below.

Part of that training process is to allow the guide to make sure you're emotionally prepared for doing this. Climbing a peak like the Grand Teton is more than just a fun adventure. It's also dangerous. People can die doing it. To me, that was a little intimidating.

We passed the test.

The first day of the ascent is a long hike up to about 11,000 feet, where Exum maintains a base camp. It's a beautiful hike through a high-elevation western evergreen forest full of spruce, aspen, pine, and alpine fir as slender as church steeples. Where the trail passed lakes or beaver ponds or crossed creeks, we saw moose. We saw elk and deer in the meadows, and eagles and hawks soared overhead.

As we hiked, our guide confronted me about an attitude he'd been picking up on—the truth is I was apprehensive, you might even say fearful, about this climb. To be honest, I found myself thinking more than once, *What the heck am I doing? I've got four kids! I've read the stories about people who've been killed on this climb! What was I thinking when I put this trip together?*

Our guide didn't have to be a mind-reader to pick up on my fears as we hiked along—I'm sure it was written on my face and audible in my voice. At one point we stopped and sat on some granite boulders for a short rest, and he said, "I need to tell you something. You need to make a decision that you're going to make this climb before you get to base camp. Because when you get there you're going to look up at the Grand, and it'll look like a massive granite spire that sticks straight up higher than you can imagine, and you'll feel intimidated. If you have the tiniest doubt in your mind that you can do it as you're hiking up there today, then once you stand at base camp tonight and look up, you'll be convinced that you can't possibly climb that thing. So today as we're hiking up, you need to decide whether you're going to go through with this. I need to know your answer before we get there."

And Jessica who, with the courage of the young, had no fear about any of this, was a real encouragement. "Dad, we can do this," she said. "Don't worry about it. Let's just do it."

She was right. I made up my mind that no matter how many second thoughts I had when I got to base camp, no matter how unconquerable the Grand Teton looked from there, I was all in.

The trees grew steadily smaller and more contorted as we made our way higher, and then we were above tree line, surrounded only by rocks, grass, and vast empty slopes. Other than birds, the only wildlife were marmots (like a high-elevation, dark-red groundhog) and pikas (resembling a cross between a rabbit and a hamster) that foraged for grass among the boulders. The trail is steep and rocky at that point, but it's still a hike as opposed to a climb—you're just carrying a lot of heavy equipment.

We huffed and puffed into the base camp maintained by Exum Mountain Guides at over 11,000 feet in the saddle between the Grand Teton and the Middle Teton. I dropped my pack with relief and gratitude, looked up at the Grand Teton, and thought, once again, *What am I doing up here? Why did I decide to do this? Am I out of my mind?* But I knew why I'd come. And I knew why it was important. And I had already decided. I was committed. No turning back.

The base camp is nestled down among the boulders. The main building looks like a Quonset hut. There were about twenty people at the base camp that night, all planning to ascend the peak the next day—the same day we were. Twenty men—and one sixteen-year-old girl. Our guide set up a tent for Jessica and me beside the main hut, so that she wouldn't have to sleep in a hostel-type arrangement with twenty men she'd never met.

We'd carried our sleeping bags up the mountain, and Jessica and I had air mattresses in the tent the guides had set up for us. Food consisted mostly of energy bars, jerky, and similar types of food that didn't need preparation, but we ate lots of it to provide energy. You spent the evening setting up, checking your gear, meeting people—just hanging out, drinking the coffee prepared by the guides. There's a lot of nervous anticipation. You're all watching the weather, because, as you know if you've watched any movies about mountain climbing, it's all about weather.

I woke up about two in the morning and, braving the wind that had been howling outside all night long, left the tent to go to the rough latrine. After all, you drink a lot of water at that elevation because the air is thin. Walking toward the latrine, I stopped dead in amazement—the stars at 11,000 feet, above the air pollution and with much of the atmosphere and all of the lights of civilization below us, are stunning and indescribable. I was so glad that there were no clouds—just countless stars, more stars than I'd ever thought could exist. *And,* I thought, *this should mean clear skies in the morning—and good weather for our ascent.*

Our guide woke us up about 4:00 a.m. "If you guys hurry, we can be the first ones on the route."

We grabbed our gear, ate quickly, and took off—once again fighting the wind that lasted all day.

Everything was new to me. We wore headlamps as we walked out of base camp because at that hour, even at 11,000 feet, it was completely dark—and it remained that way for the first hour or two of the ascent. We weren't yet to the technical part of the climb—it was still primarily a hike. But by the time dawn began to brighten the sky to a dull gray-blue, we were beginning the technical part.

The climb progressed slowly, methodically, through a series of multiple pitches in which the guide moves up the rock face fifty to seventy feet. When he stops and calls back down, the second person climbs the same distance, using the rope and the climbing techniques our guide taught us. Then the third person climbs the same distance. That's one pitch. Then the guide sets out again, setting up the next pitch.

It's a very calculated, meticulous, steady, incredibly exhilarating process. And even though we'd never climbed this mountain before (or any mountain, for that matter), we felt a certain sense of familiarity with each pitch anyway, because of the reading and preparation we'd done. The reading, of course, doesn't begin to prepare you for what it's really like. And when you find yourself suddenly there in the very places you'd read about, the very places you'd seen in photos, the sense of exhilaration is incredible.

We climbed for hours, slowly but surely making our way up the face of the mountain. It may have been meticulous and slow, but there was nothing routine about it, and as exciting as it was, it was also frightening. Mountain climbers use the term *exposure* to refer to how far you would fall at any point if, despite the safety precautions, you lost your grip and went into freefall. A twenty-foot exposure means that from the spot you are on the mountain, if you were to actually fall off, you would fall twenty feet.

At one point in this climb, we had to traverse Wall Street—the name climbers have given to a particular ledge across the rock face. It grew steadily narrower and narrower until it finally seems as if it's only a foot wide, and even allowing for exaggeration, it couldn't have been more than eighteen inches. To make matters worse, there's a gap in the ledge, a place where you have to step across nothingness to reach the continuation of the ledge on the far side.

Our guide told us as we approached the ledge that our exposure from that ledge was a thousand feet—a good reason to make that crossing roped up, which we did. "The best way to cross this ledge," he told us, "is to face the cliff, step sideways, and keep your eyes focused on the rocks six inches in front of your face. And don't *ever* look down."

Jessica was going to cross the ledge before me. Just before she stepped onto it, she looked back at me and said, "Dad, are you okay?"

I nodded.

And then she turned and slowly, carefully crossed it. When she was secure, she looked back at me and said, "Just look at the rocks in front of your face, Dad. You can do this."

I was moved. Here was my daughter, the one I'd been thinking of as vulnerable and in need for the past few months, giving me the strength to do something I was afraid to do— and I was definitely afraid to do this. I almost couldn't gather the courage to attempt it. That may have been the first time in our lives where she was the one getting me through something rather than the other way around.

One thing the guide hadn't mentioned is that when you come to that gap in the ledge, you *have* to look down to make sure you put your foot in a secure place. I looked down a thousand feet through that gap. It was a long way. And nothing but jagged rocks below.

I made it across.

Somewhere between 12,000 and 13,000 feet in elevation, we reached the section of the climb called the Golden Staircase. It was an incredible moment: The sun was just cresting the horizon, and the view was spectacular. The route we were climbing progresses right up the face of the ridge, very airy and exposed, and absolutely beautiful. Jessica was climbing below me, and at one point she yelled up and said, "Dad, we're on the Golden Staircase!"

Yes, we are, I thought, *and in more ways than simply the name of this unforgettable pitch on this mountain.* "Look behind you," I yelled. "Did you ever think you'd look *down* on the Middle Teton?"

The Middle Teton is the third-highest peak in the entire Teton Range, and from the Golden Staircase we were actually above it, looking down on it across a vast expanse. In fact, from where we were, everything we saw was a great distance away with nothing but crystalline air between us.

We were so focused on our climb—on using good technique, on being careful and deliberate, that when the climb began to level out a bit, we didn't really notice. At least, not until our guide stopped, turned around, and said, "So—we can't go any higher."

I didn't get it at first. "You mean—are we at the top?"

He smiled and nodded. "This is it."

The summit of the Grand Teton is a flat area filled with boulders. After all that concentration, all of that effort, all of that anticipation, Jessica and I couldn't believe we were there.

And there was no one else there but our guide—by getting an early start, we had made it up before any of the other teams. The three of us sat on boulders, and Jessica and I kept repeating variations of, "Can you believe it? We did it! We're at the top of the Grand Teton!"

The moment was incredibly meaningful for Jessica after all she'd been through, all she had risked, and to now be well on the road to recovery. But that moment possessed a particularly powerful meaning for me, too: I had looked up at, admired, and stood in awe of this mountain for much of my life, after first falling in love with it at eighteen. But I had always seen it only from various angles back on the valley floor. Now I was standing on the peak. On the valley floor, my attention had been focused on the peak. But now, standing on the peak, I had gained a vantage point from which to enjoy the rest of the world—or at least so it felt.

Where would I even begin in describing the symbolic value of that moment—of the effort we had put into the climb, of the victory we (especially Jessica) had gained? I had been too busy climbing for most of the day, too committed to keeping myself and Jessica safe in an exhilarating but dangerous effort, to spare many brain cells for ruminating on the meaning of the climb. But now that we were on the summit taking a short breather, I saw the climb as another example of the bittersweet nature of the lives Jessica and I and the rest of our family had lived over the past few years since Carol Ann's death. We'd worked hard and felt a lot of pain in training. And then we had invested huge amounts of effort and had to overcome (at least I did) a significant amount of fear and reluctance, and we had risked our safety in a hugely difficult climb from which a fall would have meant injury or death. Those were the bitter. But we had done it, and now a long, intense look around us was enough to convince us that we would never forget that moment and never see the world in quite the same way again. We would always have a heightened sense of its beauty and its vastness. We were seeing the world in a way only those willing and able to do what we had done could see it. And that's the sweet.

I had discussed with our guide why Jessica and I were making this trip and the importance it held for us. I'd also shared with him our family's history of the past few years. So he knew that this was an especially meaningful moment for us, and he stood and said, "I'll just hike a couple hundred yards down the mountain and leave you guys alone. You might not have long before the rest start showing up."

So for several minutes, Jessica and I had the peak of the Grand Teton completely to ourselves. It was remarkable—a father-and-daughter moment for the ages. We prayed. We thanked God that we had been able to make it up the mountain that day, but we also thanked him that despite everything, we had survived to make it to where we were in our lives.

Over three million people visit Grand Teton National Park every year, but at that moment Jessica and I were the only ones privileged to see it from the top of the Grand Teton. It made me think of what I had told my kids many, many times after their mom died: "What we're going through is terrible. But we'll survive it—and having gone through it, you'll understand things that the vast majority of kids, those who've never had to go through this, will never understand. And therefore, as adults, you will understand things that most adults won't understand. Having been forced to flex and strengthen your emotional muscles in this unwanted experience, you'll be stronger than most people. We didn't choose this, we don't want it—but it will make us better and stronger."

It's a principle my family has experienced time and again:

It's me enduring gasoline, chiggers, thorns, and sweltering heat to pick blackberries—but then being able to eat the blackberry cobbler afterward.

It's Carol Ann losing a baby, Cynthia Kate—but coming out of the depressed period afterward with a new commitment to living her life with generosity and compassion toward others, and having her life changed because of it.

It's being able to experience joy only to the level of intensity that you've already experienced sorrow.

It's the Bible telling us in the book of James, "Consider it pure joy, my brothers and sisters, whenever you face trials of many kinds..."

We had no choice about losing Carol Ann. Jessica and I *had* had a choice about climbing the Grand, and we'd chosen hard work over ease, facing our fears over running away, persevering over giving up. And this view from the Grand Teton, this cool alpine air, this vastness, was our reward. We had gained the view from the top. We could still have enjoyed the park even if we'd stayed at the bottom. Millions do. But the view from the top is reserved for those who grit their teeth and walk through the fire.

That mountaintop experience was a significant turning point—certainly for me, and I know for Jessica as well. So much had happened in our lives in the previous two years. If life comes in chapters, then with that successful climb we had brought one chapter to a close and readied ourselves for the next chapter. A mountain had been climbed. A journey had been completed. How should we memorialize it?

Fortunately, we had come prepared. Jessica had brought the suicide note she had written that terrifying day that now seemed years in the past. She pulled out a cigarette lighter she'd brought for the purpose, and she burned it.

Then I took out of my pack something I'd brought, something that signified the journey I was on: a big lock of her mother's hair. And we each took some and tossed it into the wind. We prayed.

It was a powerful, profound, and meaningful moment for the two of us.

There's more to the story. We took a different route down the peak and in one place had to rappel a hundred feet down a sheer rock face. We didn't hit base camp again on the way down—we hiked all the way to the bottom of the mountain, and the day that began at 4:00 a.m. didn't end until late afternoon, with both of us exhausted.

But for me, as enjoyable as the rest of the trip had been for both of us, the scene we shared on the peak, just the two of us, is the climax of the trip, the scene my mind always goes back to when I think of our Grand Teton adventure: father and daughter on the roof of the world, nothing between us and heaven, arms around each other, watching the ashes of a suicide note and the wisps of hair of the remarkable woman whose life we had been privileged to share for a too-brief period of time blowing away in the strong, alpine wind.

Our lives are books that contain many chapters. Some chapters of our lives we wish would last forever but they end anyway, sometimes leaving us bereft. Other chapters we're eager to see finish so that we can move on, and we shake the dust off our feet as we leave them behind. The life of the Lee family has included both types. And there's something that the good chapters and the tragic ones have in common: They come to an end—clearing the way for a new chapter to begin.

And for Jessica, and Jacob and Caleb, and Sarah Kate, for Maria and Bill, there's one thing we know for certain about the future: The chapters of our lives yet to come will be built upon the pain and the struggle we endured in the past, the joy we experienced along with that pain, and the assurance that God will walk alongside us every step.

The person who leads in life is the person who isn't afraid to face the bitter, who embraces the climb, and who knows and trusts his guide and follows his lead to gain the view from the top.

EPILOGUE

O n a beautiful late fall day in October of 2000, I walked slowly up the hill behind our house and made my way through the old iron fence my dad and I had bought from an antique shop to enclose our family cemetery. The graves there actually predate our family's buying this land—there are tombstones in this cemetery over 150 years old. But we've made it ours now, and there have been a few Lee graves added to the older ones already here.

A cool breeze rustled the leaves as I sat in the sun on the bench some of Carol Ann's friends donated not long after Carol Ann's funeral, with their names inscribed on it. Someone else had donated a tree that now shaded the spot where we'd laid her body just three months before. It was buried there now in its coffin, covered by a concrete base—but no tombstone. Not yet. I was here today to watch its installation.

I looked back over my shoulder, up the hill. I could see, not far away, a place that held painful memories for me: the spot where she and our daughter Sarah Kate had been thrown from Carol Ann's horse Bar just three months before. Ironic, I guess, that she was buried within sight of the spot where she'd died. Ironic, or perhaps just appropriate. She'd lived here and died here, and now she was buried here. It was a beautiful spot to sit and remember her.

Often I came here just to sit on the bench and think about Carol Ann and our life together and everything her life had meant and had accomplished. And perhaps to put flowers on her grave. But today I had an additional purpose, and judging from the pickup I now saw making its way up the hill, that purpose was soon to be accomplished. The pickup rolled to a stop near the iron fence, and a couple of older workers in gray work clothes climbed out. They were here to deliver and install the tombstone I'd ordered to sit on the base over Carol Ann's grave.

The marker was a marble Celtic cross with the four kids' names on the circle. And Proverbs 31:29:

"Many women do noble things,
but you surpass them all."

And in the middle, a sunflower with seeds falling.

The two men installed the stone and drove away. And I sat there in the sunshine on that mild fall day looking at it. There's something surreal about seeing a cemetery marker of someone you love. We had survived the trauma of her death, we had suffered through her funeral, we had done our best to come to terms with her absence from our lives who had been such a central and loving part of it. But when you see the funeral marker, there it is, carved in stone. Her name: Carol Ann Lee. More than a name to me—it was the sound of her voice, heard no longer. The fragrance of her skin, now just a memory. It was the wisdom she brought to our marriage and to the raising of our kids, wisdom that now I had to maneuver through life without.

The date of her birth: August 7, 1959.

And the date of her death, just three months ago, a day that, along with the three days before it, from the hour of her accident, I could relive in minute detail: July 22, 2000.

I remember thinking, *Wow. She's in heaven. I wonder what she's doing right now.* And a second question came almost as fast: *What would she say to me if she could?*

People who have a relationship with God have unique ways of hearing from him. The way God speaks to me is difficult to describe but when it happens, it's undeniable. What I felt him say that morning in the cemetery was, *If she could speak to you now, she would tell you that there are only a few things in life that really matter. One is that you know me. Another is whether anyone else in the world knows me because of your life.*

Those were deep thoughts, and I sat and considered them— and the long list of other things in my life that, perhaps, I cared about more than I should. I stared at her marker as I thought. And I realized that I will have my own cemetery marker in this same little cemetery, close to Cynthia Kate's, across from Mr. and Mrs. Linton's. It might be forty days from now, it might be forty years, but it will be soon. And on the day the stone is placed there with my name on it, I too will care about a few things far more than anything else.

I sat alone for another hour or so in the breeze in that beautiful spot, then stood to leave. The bitter finality of that day—a marker, a grave, a memory—had been transformed in my mind and heart into a sweet impression to live my life poured out for those things that matter. Into a reminder that I had four kids to raise, a company to grow, and grandchildren to dream about. Into a reminder that my dad was right—life really is short. And into a conviction that there were very few things that matter, and I need to be about those things.

It's been many years since that afternoon. I have spent many of those years trying to live out that conviction. The years have been, like all of life's journey, bitter and sweet. There is now a marker in that cemetery with my dad's name on it, a reminder of the brevity of life. *Life is short,* his marker should read. But there have been an abundance of sweet days as well, days that overshadowed the bitterness.

My children are adults now, happy and godly, each at different stages of life and each with joys and struggles of their own. But each richly blessed and full of hope.

Maria came into my life just as the skies were clearing. And what she has brought to me for the past ten years has been a new level of joy and love and devotion that was difficult for me to even imagine in those cloudiest of days. While much of this story has revolved around loss and pain, my story today is not about the past but about a solid hope for the future that, rather than being quashed by my experiences, has been magnified by them.

Maria and I are enjoying those grandchildren I dreamed about, my company has grown to levels I had hardly dared hope for, my children have futures even brighter than mine—and I'm convicted all the more to be about those things that matter.

Have I always stayed true to that calling? Of course not. I am a flawed man who has made plenty of mistakes and often missed the mark. But that's the beauty of a real relationship with God. He gives grace and forgiveness for our weaknesses and failures, and strength and courage to begin anew.

This road I'm on is headed to a place that I can only imagine. But along the way there's room for a life that is rich and full of laughter and joy, pain and sorrow, life and death, reward and disappointment. It's bitter and it's sweet.

And I'm more convinced than ever that bittersweet is the most wonderful flavor of all.